Why? Why Not? Why Don't We?

This book is based on the inaugural speech by Winy Maas at October 15, 2009 to mark the acceptance of the Chair of Architecture and Urban Design at the Faculty of Architecture of the Delft University of Technology, the opening of the Why Factory in Delft by Dutch Minister of Education and Culture Ronald Plasterk and the symposium "My Future City", where a variety of students, inhabitants, architects, urbanists, thinkers, developers, politicians, technicians offer their future city…

Table of Content

1	**The Why Factor(y) and The Future City**	
	Winy Maas	
1.1	**Welcome to Your Future**	
1.2	**The Why Factor**	
1.2.1		Why Why?
1.2.2		Intimidating Crises
1.2.3		The Wider Agenda
1.2.4		Scale
1.2.5		Communicative Architecture
1.2.6		The Larger Potential
1.2.7		Conclusion: Architecture as Tests
1.2.8		The Iconic
1.2.9		Architecture is a Device
1.3	**The Why Factory**	
1.3.1		Why A Factory?
1.3.2		Delft
1.3.3		Public Private Partnership
1.3.4		Research Units
1.3.5		Thin Line
1.3.6		The Mini Schools
1.4	**The Tribune**	
1.4.1		The Rainbow Tower
1.4.2		The Fire
1.4.3		The Nomadic Period
1.4.4		The New Building: a Collection of Interpretations
1.4.5		The Orange Tribune
1.5	**The Future City**	
1.5.1		Introduction
1.5.2		The Tripod
1.5.3		The Modelcities Program
1.5.3.1		The Green Dream
1.5.3.2		New Worldwonders
1.5.3.3		The Death of Leisure
1.5.4		The Applications Program
1.5.4.1		Rtm 2050
1.5.4.2		Hongkong Fantasies
1.5.4.3		Nl To Do
1.5.4.4		The Vertical Village©
1.5.4.5		City Pig
1.5.4.6		Foodprint Manhattan

1.5.5		The Software Program
1.5.5.1		Spacefighter©
1.5.5.2		The Green City Calculator©
1.5.5.3		The Village Maker©
1.6		**Conclusions and Acknowledgements**
2		**The Why Factory Opening**
2.1		When You Make Cities, You Are Making Lifes
		Ronald Plasterk
3		**My Future City Is… (1)**
		Interviews by *Tihamér Salij* with *Bas Kalmeijer*, *Ania Molenda* and *Ryan Forster*
4		**My Future City Is… (2)**
4.1		**Future Cities Are Not About Stones, They Are About People**
		Bas Verkerk
4.2		**Bring Poor And Rich Together…**
		Coen Van Oostrom
4.3		**My Future City Is Located In My Imagination**
		Kristin Feirreis
4.4		**A City That Symbolizes The Will Of Mankind**
		Bernhard Hufenbach
4.5		**Nature Invites Buildings And Invades Buildings**
		Rob Nijsse
4.6		**Design And The Designer Have To Enter Fearless And Aggressively Into The Arena**
		Henk Ovink
4.7		**My System Will Increase Competition Between Cities**
		Ronald Wall
4.8		**Young People Are The City Of Virtue Of Tomorrow**
		Ole Bouman
4.9		**We Do Not Believe In Big Plans, We Belive In Creating Facts On The Ground**
		Wouter Vanstiphout
4.10		**In My Future, 'Flowerpower' Will Become Productive**
		Pirjo Haikola
4.11		**The Why Factory Needs Another Name**
		Michiel Riedijk
4.12		**Freedom Of Decision Is Something That Belongs To You**
		Frank Bijdendijk
4.13		**In 2034, the Why Factory Has Been Franchised All Around The World**
		Jacob Van Rijs and *Nathalie De Vries*
4.14		**Don't Focus On Answers But On Questions**
		Wytze Patijn

4

1.
The Why Factor(y)
and The Future City

1.1. Welcome to Your Future

Mijnheer de Rector Magnificus, leden van het College van Bestuur, Collegae hoogleraren en andere leden van de universitaire gemeenschap, zeer gewaardeerde toehoorders, Dames en heren.

Mr. Plasterk, Minister of Culture and Education of the Netherlands, Mr. Verkerk, Mayor of the City of Delft, Mr. Fokkema, Rector Magnificus of the Delft University of Technology, Mr. Patyn, Wytze, Dean of the Faculty of Architecture, dear colleagues, dear family, dear friends, dear ladies and gentlemen and last but certainly not least dear students.

I want to welcome you all to The Why Factory, a research platform and urbanistic think-tank that, through fundamental architectural research and argumentation, explore the possibilities for the development of our cities.

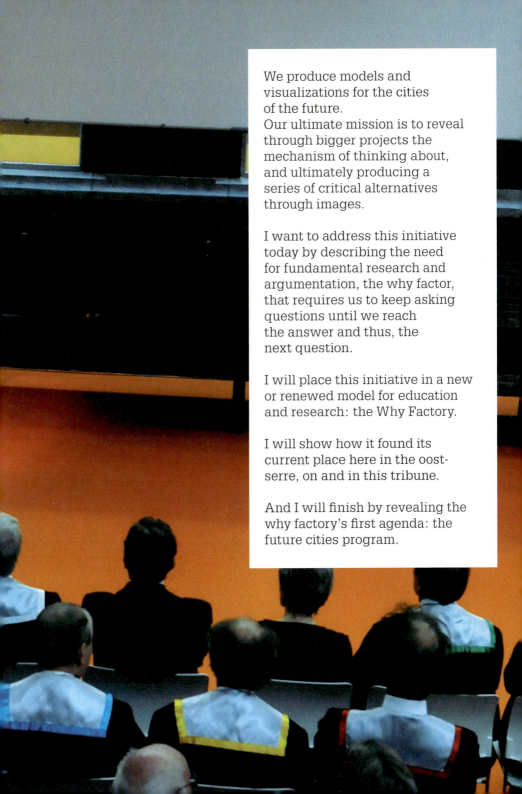

We produce models and visualizations for the cities of the future.
Our ultimate mission is to reveal through bigger projects the mechanism of thinking about, and ultimately producing a series of critical alternatives through images.

I want to address this initiative today by describing the need for fundamental research and argumentation, the why factor, that requires us to keep asking questions until we reach the answer and thus, the next question.

I will place this initiative in a new or renewed model for education and research: the Why Factory.

I will show how it found its current place here in the oost-serre, on and in this tribune.

And I will finish by revealing the why factory's first agenda: the future cities program.

1.2. The Why Factor

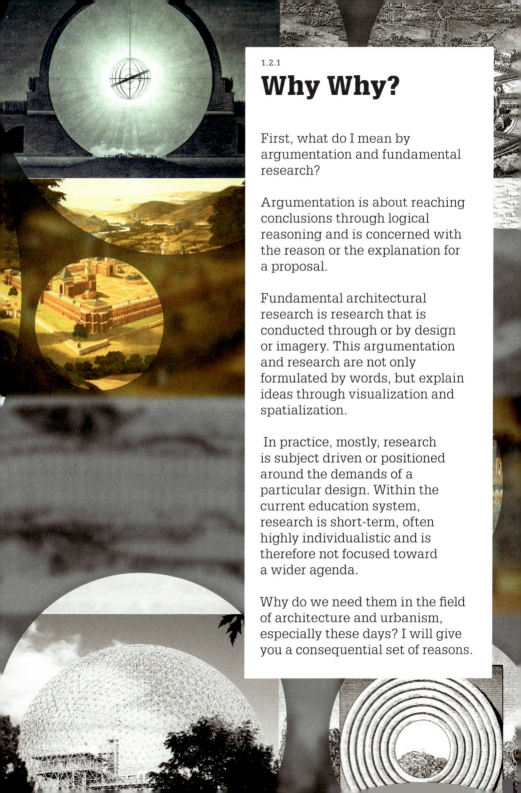

1.2.1
Why Why?

First, what do I mean by argumentation and fundamental research?

Argumentation is about reaching conclusions through logical reasoning and is concerned with the reason or the explanation for a proposal.

Fundamental architectural research is research that is conducted through or by design or imagery. This argumentation and research are not only formulated by words, but explain ideas through visualization and spatialization.

In practice, mostly, research is subject driven or positioned around the demands of a particular design. Within the current education system, research is short-term, often highly individualistic and is therefore not focused toward a wider agenda.

Why do we need them in the field of architecture and urbanism, especially these days? I will give you a consequential set of reasons.

1.2.2
Intimidating Crises

"In uncertain times, despair seems to enter architecture. Faced with political, cultural or economic crises (Some say that we even have a culture of crises that actually helps us to navigate through eternity…), many architects behave like rather opportunistic ostriches who neglect, within an environment that is dominated by fear, any alternatives. Accumulating frustration leads to skepticism if not cynicism, that diminish the architect's position. It turns the role of the architect more and more into a pure service provider, as demonstrated in the increasing appearances of corporate architectural offices in the world. This fear ultimately gives also space for a re-historic architecture of nostalgia that, with its backward looking answer kills curiosity and experimentation, the source of innovation and progress. How conscious and argumentative are these positions? Or better said: how relevant are they? How short term oriented?
So: how visionary are they?

1.2.3
The Wider Agenda

In the best cases some architects choose minimalism to escape from the overkill of information images. While others choose for 'shapiness', that offers maybe some intriguing mystery but lack revelation…
Enormous reductionism seems to appear. The youngest generation of architects does not believe in visions or better-said wider perspectives and concentrate on small, beautiful, relatively autonomous objects. The key question arises if architecture should only concentrate on its autonomous components as space, light, and composition? Or can it use the built up knowledge on these matters for a wider context?
"Can't we thus use architecture to put itself more consciously in the middle of the public debate on space? Space accommodates current and future political, economic, and societal demands. Architects can actively visualize this process and thus comment on it.
But it demands for a tremendous argumentative intelligence."

1.2.4
Scale

But architecture is also intimidated by large scale.
The enormous production of urban matter has dwarfed the urban and architectural intervention.
The demand and desire to live in suburban conditions have stretched the cities' boundaries. Even up till the moment that the classical cities touch the next one. And the landscapes, in between or what is left over of that, have become a stronger functional part of the cities for its food and oxygen. The world has become one city. How to respond with our objects and interventions, even the smallest ones, towards this scale?
"It requires a strong argumentative combination of research and practice."

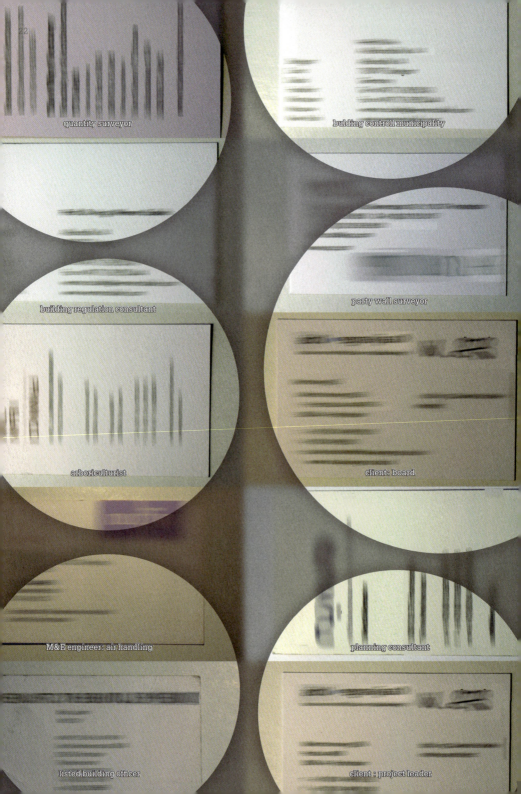

1.2.5

Communicative Architecture

In the mean time, the current complicated process of realizing buildings and cities, asks for collaborations. With engineers, politicians, users, citizens. We all are becoming building-makers and town planners. In this palette of specialists, the architect becomes the spatial specialist. "This affects architecture as it demands a communicative process oriented architectural language that is direct, de-mystified, understandable. This language stretches beyond classical categories of form, shape and light, while not neglecting them. It keeps up with the need for passion, intrigue and surprise, but positions them in a wider perspective."

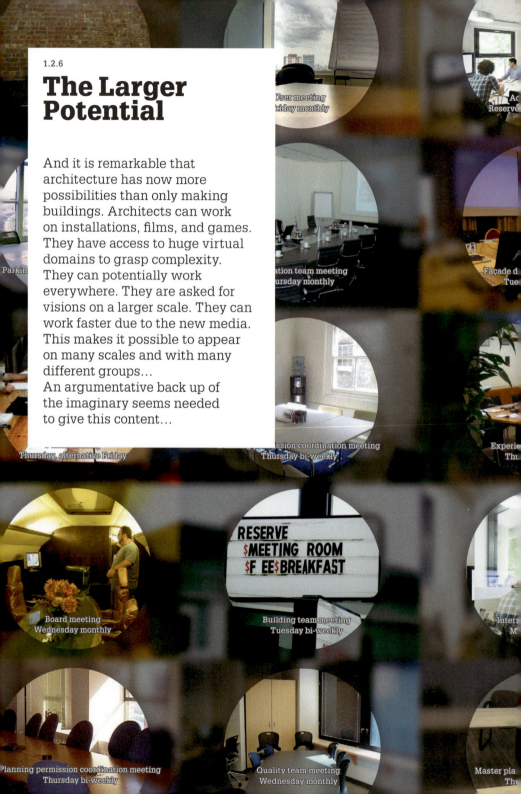

1.2.6
The Larger Potential

And it is remarkable that architecture has now more possibilities than only making buildings. Architects can work on installations, films, and games. They have access to huge virtual domains to grasp complexity. They can potentially work everywhere. They are asked for visions on a larger scale. They can work faster due to the new media. This makes it possible to appear on many scales and with many different groups…
An argumentative back up of the imaginary seems needed to give this content…

1.2.7

Conclusion: Architecture as Tests

How can architecture embody all that? How can all this turn into projects?

"We can propose that, relatively small projects, architecture, can be seen as tests, stressing their exemplary role, acting as a pars pro toto, or a pièce de resistance. Their constructions can be considered as temporarily "petrifactions" of these wider scale (r)evolutions.
They ultimately can turn wider demands into icons that communicate to a wider audience, outside the typical architectural circle."

1.2.8
The Iconic

Icons are under severe attack. Recently every city wants an icon. And actually they all want the same. Cities thus start to collect instead of to invent. These are not icons any more.
Where it used to be a tool for enlightened mayors to show important directions, they now start to be interpreted as personal megalomanias. This critic is illustrative for societies where increased individualistic aspects shift the collective away, or to other zones. How to make exemplary projects and buildings in that context? That impress, that wonder, that explore, that guide… How to make new icons in that respect?
We definitely need a criticism on icons.

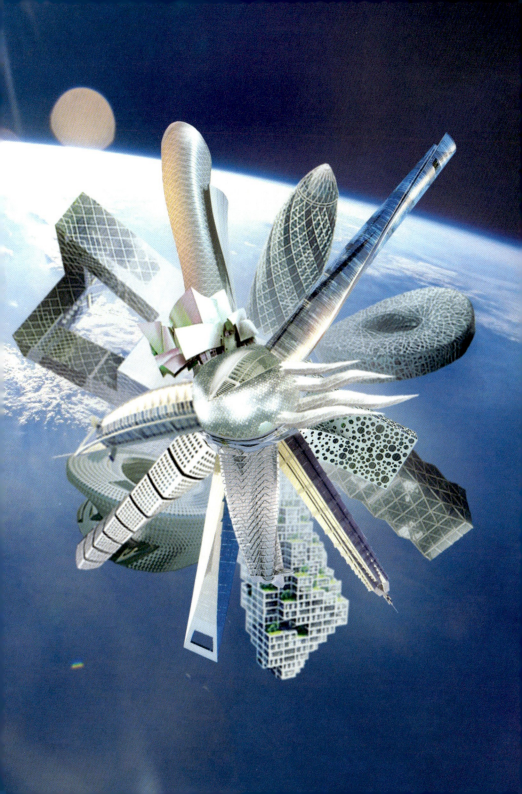

Architecture is a device

Winy Maas, 2004

Unification? Is it true that in no other eve[nt] than the design competition for Ground Z[ero] have so many architects from such differ[ent] backgrounds – former enemies, so to s[peak] – tried to work on the same topics? The [?] towers that branched, kissed, split a[nd] hovered – aimed to produce urban lif[e] up by increasing densities, accepting and aspiring to a global future where people will inhabit the planet. In an [?] communal enterprise, blob and dat[a] merged with rationalists and super[?] Does the Ground Zero competition demonstrate that a shared idealism emerged among architects despi[te] [?] unitary obsessions? It [?]sents a new

1.2.9

Architecture is a Device

With all this, architecture is now able to become "devices" that combine top-down, large-scale issues with bottom-up, individualized input: a combination of analyses with proposals. Consequently, its products can be understood as "instruments" of general observations, as "messengers" of urban transactions and criticism, as "facilitators" for development and acceleration and as "communicators" of wider processes and agendas. A device is more than a tool, it is more than an instrument, and it is more than a movement. It is societal and instrumental, critical, and cultural. It motivates and broadens research and it provides a mechanism for exploration of models and visualizations.

This 'devicing' deserves subsequent argumentation so that it can give architecture more meaning, and make it more critical, deep and profound.
And not only in words. We need images, buildings and an architecture that can be by itself argumentative, expressing this content to a wider audience.

1.3. The Why Factory

1.3.1

Why a Factory?

This argumentative research needs a series of tests. Maybe even a production line of thoughts and counter-thoughts… in words, but mainly in images. This cannot be covered in a short-term studio. It demands a longer-term operation. The Why Factory is our answer to this.

The Why Factory is not just a name, but it is a description of how the whole program operates.

The 'Why' gets to the core of the message, the heart of the content of the architectural or urbanistic proposal. Is questioning not the university's core business? They should go to down to the bone, and they should be endless. After one hypothesis the next one is always revealed.
And just to be clear: obviously a simplified argumentation needs to be avoided. This 'why factor' needs to integrate also a 'why not factor': intuition, feelings and beauty,…

The factory is about production. This accelerates and even models the sequence of thoughts and anti-thoughts. It simulates an evolutionary process. This replaces the current scenario thinking, based on hypotheses, the 'what if's', with a more inter-reactive chain thinking: the 'yes but'. That is embodied in the Why Factory.

Can this be accommodated within the existing university system?

1.3.1
Delft

When I was asked in 2005 by the former dean, Hans Beunderman, to apply for this chair, I initially hesitated. For many students and scholars Delft was (or is) not sexy. It had maybe the glamour of the past, and it is surrounded by great contemporary Dutch architects, but is not like the AA, the Bartlett, Harvard, Princeton, the ETH and others that all have their remarkabilities. And Delft? What speciality does it have?

First, it has size. Delft has a substantial amount of students, which is very attractive because different research schools can be applied much more easily than at a smaller institution.
Secondly, it is simply surrounded by a generation of top tier, globally oriented architects.

And the third opportunity that Delft opens up, comes from what others might see as an obstacle... Delft has almost no unifying vision at the moment. But that also means that a vision is needed and so there is a ground to do it.
It is time to formulate a more distinctive position for this university within a world of universities and architectural departments.

Research sinusoid
Winy Maas, 2005

In the book Km3 Excursions on Capacity I noticed that "Many graduate and postgraduate programs in universities are developed by and concentrated in studio work: these are short-term design programs that do not allow for fundamental research." There is often no urge or obligation for publication…
For many specialists (like architects and urban planners) it becomes unattractive to teach in universities due to this. Running a studio for a semester does not equate with the ambitions that could be placed elsewhere, as in practice.

Maybe research seems to flourish best when it is considered a clear project with a considerable, but not too long, time span: for example, say, five years? In such a period a "project" can be conceived, tested and publicized.

Such a more subject driven research unit, in analogy with other academic domains as medicine and natural science, can counterbalance the previously mentioned issues. The unit is run by one specialist (the professor) who leads a staff of assistants and PHD students that act as coordinators, researchers, organizers, editors and co-writers. Studios at different levels contribute to the research subject. A considerable budget for special advisors, critics, excursions, materials, conference and an eventual publication is included. With such a package, it becomes more attractive for top specialists to engage themselves with the universities again.
 And it gives participating students content, collectivity, and a public appearance. And as they can hop around by different units experiencing different approaches…"

Autumn 2002 and published under the same name by Hatje Kantz in Stuttgart, November 2002. It created a base for the development of the Accelerator, further explored in the international workshop held at the BIR in September 2002 and published in MVRDV's *Five Minutes City*, by Episode Publishers in September 2003.

Satellite schools This process opens up further developments of research units. It questions current university's architecture programs.

Many graduate and postgraduate programs in architectural faculties are developed by and concentrated in studio work: short term design programs that do not allow for fundamental research. There is no urge or obligation to publish. This discourages the sharpness and responsibility of the possible research. This system leads to a sincere lack of fundamental architectural research within the universities, which has already been noted by the European press and by European governments strongly in the last years.

In the meantime the need for fundamental research has been enlarged: advanced developments of technology, internationalization, the influence of global processes such as mobility, climate changes, migration, environmental constraints, and the enlargement of developmental scale, have all demanded answers from architectural practices.

The short-term policy of current studio systems is disconnected with reality. For ten years now, architectural studio work is mainly concentrated on form finding and software applications. A renewed contact with politicians, economics, technicians, agrarians and the academic [...] research efforts that can regain [...] and support.

For many world-class specialists (architects and urban planners) it becomes more and more impossible and unattractive to teach in universities within the current studio system. Running a studio for a semester does not give the proper output for the ambitions that could compensate the effort of travels and low wages.

On the other hand the tenure system is too slow to accommodate rapid societal changes, since sufficient vacancies are not to be expected in short time spans. This system does not allow for needed changes in subject because of its permanent character.

Research thrives when it is considered as a clear project within a considerable but not too long time span: for instance three years. In such a period a 'project' can be conceived, tested and publicized. Such a time span a[llows] for a more direct application in the architectural and urban planning practice. Such a period would even encourage the produ[ction] of the research.

For this reason, research units, in anal[ogy] with other academic domains as medi[cal] and natural science, can counterbala[nce] the issues mentioned above when ru[n by] one specialist, leading a staff of ass[istants] and PhD students that act as coord[ina]tors, researchers, organizers, edito[rs,] co-writers. Studios at different leve[ls] contribute to the research. A cons[iderable] budget for special advisors, critic[s, excur]sions, materials, conference and [publica]tion should be included.

1.3.3
Public-private Partnership

In the past, MVRDV did collaborate with other institutes as the Berlage within the practice. Can the demands to teach not be used to make a more profound research trajectory thinkable? A research unit in which MVRDV and universities participate?

1.3.4

Research Units

How to develop such research units? Of course students should 'practice' by making simulations… But architectural universities deserve more. How to make a more general agenda appearing out of the highly individualized material? Can a part of it not be dedicated to more research oriented graduation processes? Can we thus 'use' parts of the individual intelligence and talent to make more collective messages?

or instance three years,
roject' can be conceived.
d. Such a time span allows
plication in the architec-
nning practice. Such a
encourage the productivity

esearch units, in analogy
mic domains as medicine
nce, can counterbalance
oned above when run by
eading a staff of assistants
nts that act as coordina-
organizers, editors and

1.3.5

Thin Line

There is a thin line between commercial and academic premises. Can these research units maybe do what cannot be done in the commercial world: namely what is typically substantially experimental? Can we thus again truly experiment? Can the university again be a laboratory?

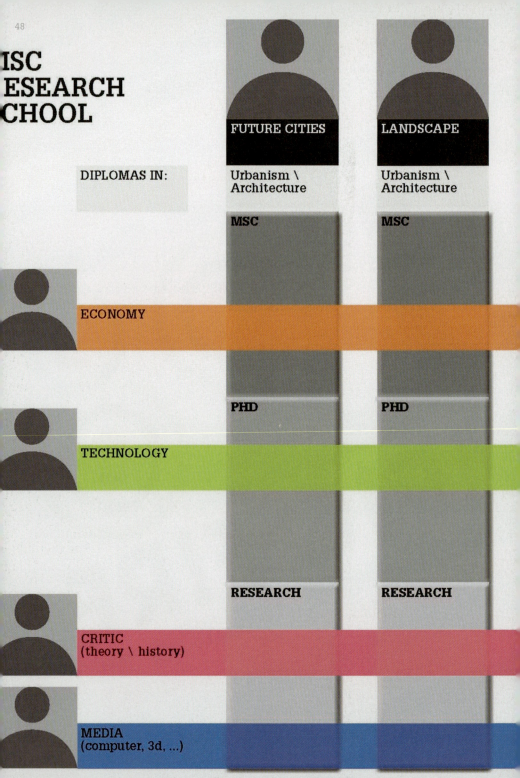

1.3.6
The Mini Schools

The recent organization with a Bachelors and a Masters school can create two characters. Where the Bsc can offer a comprehensive base, the Msc School can become a much more research driven part. The Why Factory can be seen as a start for such a construct that can contain a series of equivalent research units. 10, 15, 20? Each with a clear special subject. Each with the same budget, the same amount of students, lead by one of the great "minds" that our culture has to offer. Each very visible. A collective appearance and critic will serve these units, so that the units improve in quality and avoid doubles.

1.4. The Tribune

1.4.1

The Rainbow Tower

When we first started, there was no space available in the tower. And that lead to its reconceptualization. By imagining to dedicate every floor to a research unit, a "millefeuille" would appear.

The dean, Wytze Patijn, and his staff gave generously space for such a construct. By leaving the tower and moving into some containers they offered us the top floor.

We got rid of the cabinets, cleaned and painted it and made a red carpet: a club, a think tank on top of the building overlooking the Randstad. A pole opposite the famous "Bouwkunde" street on the ground floor, that tries to attract people to come up, enlarging the communication in the building…

And so we opened our doors, March 2008, and started discussions, colloquia, classes…

1.4.2
The Fire

And then only two months later, may 13 2008, a fire leaded to the collapse of the tower. I wondered if The Why Factory in its tower high ambition was condemned by fatality…

1.4.3
The Nomadic Period

For a year we became nomads. I started my professorship by teaching on the roof of the library... Then we moved subsequently to our office, the Berlage Institute, a tent camp... Sincere refugees. Not an easy start...

1.4.4

The new Building: a Collection of Interpretations

But new possibilities appeared that echo the thoughts on education as I expressed before. The tent camp became the testing place for a sincere BK-city with everyone having its tent. With the choice for the renovation of the old TU main building we sketched a BK city that would contain different interventions, with different architects, different professors, different handwritings.

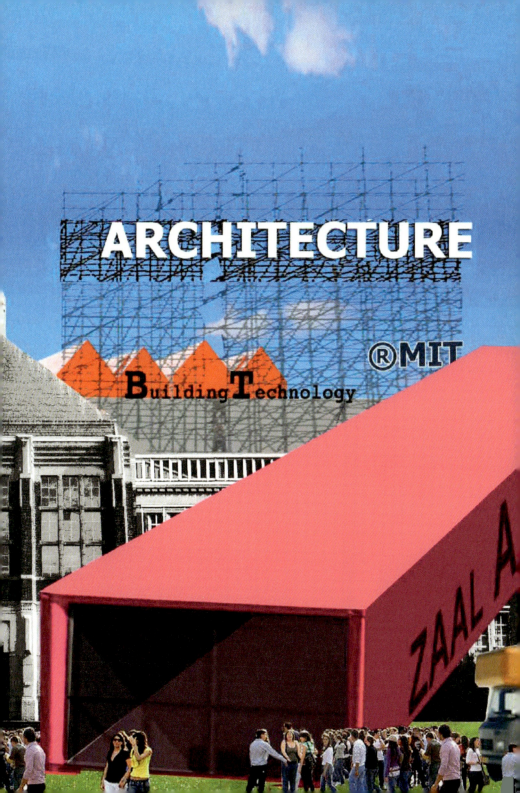

1.4.5
The Orange Tribune

The team managed to add within the limited budget two greenhouses, designed by my colleague Mick Eekhout. In one of them, in this space, MVRDV painted everything orange, a warm and welcoming environment. It includes a 'mount' in which the teachers' rooms, the presentations and meeting rooms were placed.

These rooms carry a collective tribune that can be used for performances and presentations, that becomes the central focus point in the training of future architects and urbanists: it challenges them in their public behavior and responsibility...

1.5. The Future City

1.5.1

Introduction

And here I want to introduce the first program of the factory: the future city.
Looking around the room at all of the students here, I would like to begin by taking a look forward into the world that you will graduate into. You will be entering a world where 60 per cent of the population will soon be living in cities. A world where two of the top five tourist attractions are Disney theme parks. A world where architects build only five per cent of buildings. A world where 20 'scratch-built metropolises' will emerge from deserts and rice paddies every year. A world, where in the next 25 years, the population of the world's slums will be 2.75 times the population of Europe.
How can we use architecture as a 'device' for imagining solutions for these increasingly complex global cities? How can we use our time here, to begin painting the image for both the present and the future city?
In times of uncertainty, mankind eagerly wants to know the future. In order to find new economies. In order to reveal these uncertainties and to avoid possible failures.
We can't predict the future, of course. Many predictions have failed in the past. That has caused a lot of skepticism, everywhere. But they also have steered development.

THE MODEL
The Modelcities Program

- Visionary Cities
- The Green Dream
- Worldwonders
- The Robotic City
- The Death of Leisure
- The Vertical Village
- Foodcity
- Prosper-city
- The (Un)Safest City
- NOARC: How much costs architecture?
- The extreme climates
- COPYPASTE
- Biodiver-city
- Access-city
- The Energetic City/Coolcities
- Austerity

- The Why Factor(y)/
  The Future City Program
- The Why Talks

THE VIEW
The Applications Program

- Hong Kong Fantasies
- NL To Do
- Foodprint The Hague
- Foodprint Manhattan
- NL28
- Superkampung
- Berlin 2.0
- Nomansland (Cyprus)

1.5.2
The Tripod

The future city is evidently not one city. It is built out of many future cities. Each based on its own set of parameters. In the program they are positioned in a classical research tripod of models, views and a contoller, of modelcities, applications and storage. Introduced by today's talk and accompanied in time with evaluations and discussions. Each resulting in a series of books films and games (produced by NAI press).

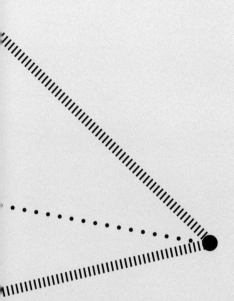

THE CONTROLLER
The Software Program

- The Green City Calculator, eu version
- The Green City Calculator, cn version
- The Spacefighter (with MIT)
- The Villagemaker

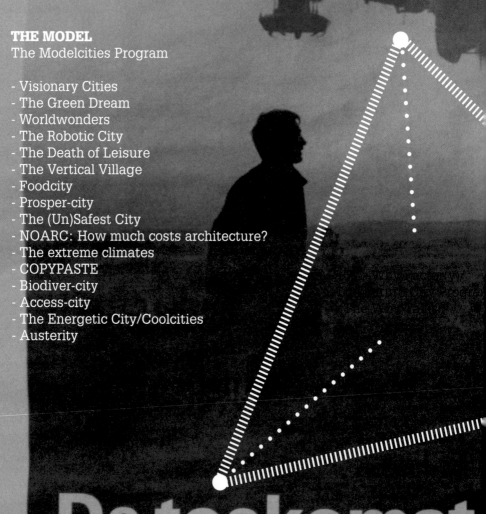

THE MODEL
The Modelcities Program

- Visionary Cities
- The Green Dream
- Worldwonders
- The Robotic City
- The Death of Leisure
- The Vertical Village
- Foodcity
- Prosper-city
- The (Un)Safest City
- NOARC: How much costs architecture?
- The extreme climates
- COPYPASTE
- Biodiver-city
- Access-city
- The Energetic City/Coolcities
- Austerity

THE VIEW
The Applications Program

- Hong Kong Fantasies
- NL To Do
- Foodprint The Hague
- Foodprint Manhattan
- NL28
- Superkamping
- Berlin 2.0
- Nomansland (Cyprus)

1.5.3
The Model City Program

In the model city program, abstract cities appear by focusing on one or two parameters that allow for maximal exploration of that specific subject. T?F seeks for a refined combination of 'science' and 'fiction'. Let me show some of them.

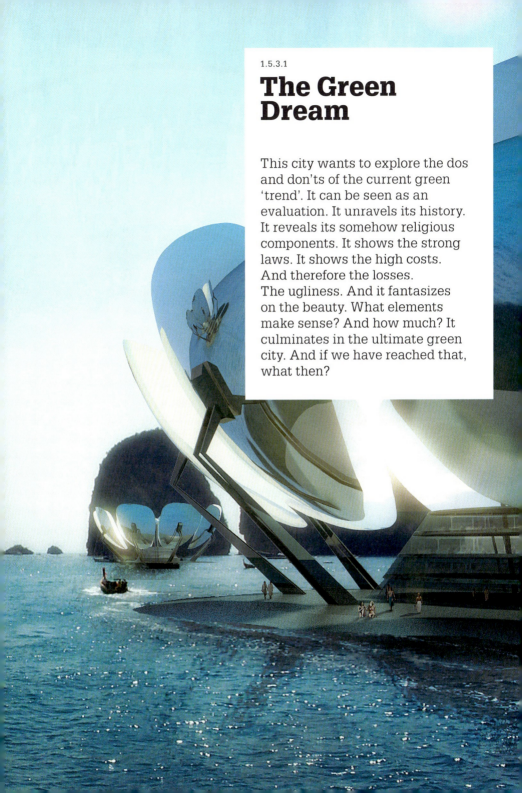

1.5.3.1

The Green Dream

This city wants to explore the dos and don'ts of the current green 'trend'. It can be seen as an evaluation. It unravels its history. It reveals its somehow religious components. It shows the strong laws. It shows the high costs. And therefore the losses. The ugliness. And it fantasizes on the beauty. What elements make sense? And how much? It culminates in the ultimate green city. And if we have reached that, what then?

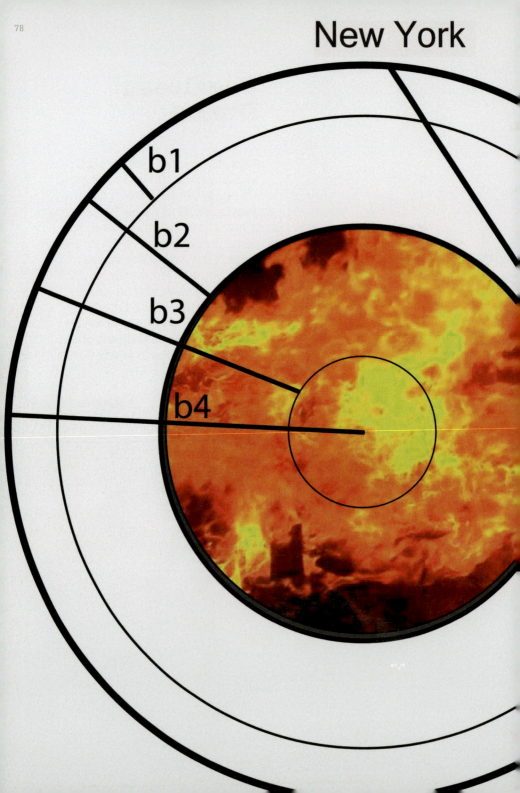

1.5.3.2

New World Wonders

In collaboration with the World Wonder Foundation, its website will be prolonged with a future chapter. What will be the new world wonders? What future architecture can be measured on world scale? Is size the only matter that counts in these lists? What tendencies can be expected? T?F speculates on the endless need and desire for wondering. Culminating in new world record's achievements.

Upper mantle	40-900	
Mantle	900-2.890	
Outer core	2.890-5.100	2.90(
Inner core	5.100-6.378	4.00(

Mumbai

1.5.3.3

The Death Of Leisure

The death of leisure project studies the leisure industry that covers nearly 20% of our economies and nearly 25% of our territories… It explores the excesses, it speculates on the beauty and horror. It dwells on the loss of exoticism, one of the major motors of this economy, and its physical and virtual replacements. And it wonders how much leisure we can actually take. When does this increasing leisure economy come to an end? When do we need to produce again?

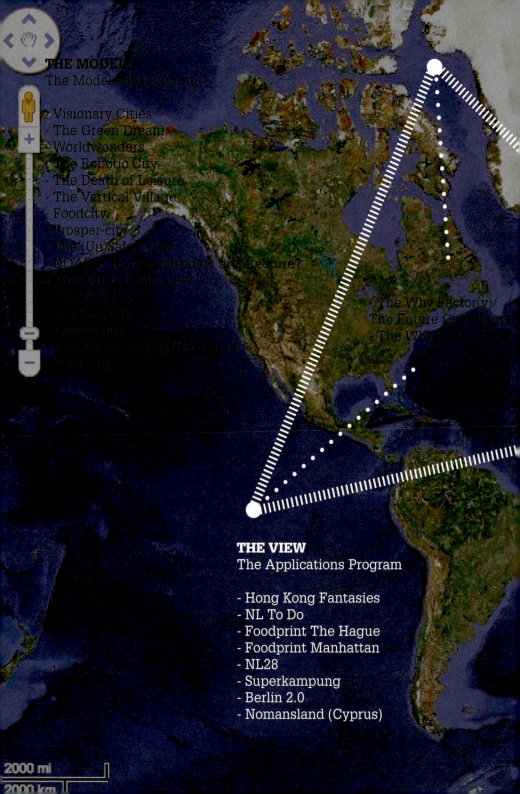

THE MODELS
The Modelcities Program

- Visionary Cities
- The Green Dream
- Worldwonders
- The Robotic City
- The Death of Leisure
- The Vertical Village
- Foodcity
- Prosper-city
- The (Un)Safe City
- NOAH / How much costs architecture?
- Poorxtremalities
- PORVETEM
- Creativecity
- Greencity
- The Bucketlist City / Modelcities
- Whatcity

THE VIEW
The Applications Program

- Hong Kong Fantasies
- NL To Do
- Foodprint The Hague
- Foodprint Manhattan
- NL28
- Superkampung
- Berlin 2.0
- Nomansland (Cyprus)

The Why Factor(y)/
The Future City Project/
The Why Factory

1.5.4

The Applications Program

In the applications program model cities both are tested in real cities. T?F collaborates with local institutions to test different hypotheses discusses them with local governments and population. I give you some examples.

THE CONTROLLER
The Software Program

The Green City Calculator, en version
The Green City Calculator, cn version
The Spacefighter (with MIT)
The Villagemaker

1.5.4.1

RTM2050

in 2007 we organized, together with a student organization, Indesem, a traditional international design seminar in Delft. As part of this seminar 20 billboards have been created in Rotterdam, to communicate possible futures of the city…

1.5.4.2

Hongkong Fantasies

With universities in Hong Kong a film has been made for the BODW in 2008, to investigate the potential of Hong Kong in its competition with the four surrounding S's: Shanghai, Shenzhen, Singapore, Seoul. Can this phenomenal city, the densest and greenest in the word, remain exemplary within this competition?

1.5.4.3

NL To Do

As part of NAI's, the Dutch national architectural institute in Rotterdam, investigation of the future of the Netherlands, some future potential disasters have been invented and investigated on its spatial implications. Cow diseases, milk pollutions, water disasters, sudden vegetal growths, traffic collapses, electricity cuts… To imagine new 'Netherlandses', and to investigate ultimately the flexibility and adaptability of the Dutch society.

International edition since 2021

Delivery: delivery@nrc.eu of 0888 5720572 Mo/Fr till 19.45, Sa/So till 16.45

Price € 1,80

nrc.eu

Europe's biggest water dam improves energy production

- Internal affairs: page 7

Neo-Maglev train reaches sound barrier

- Science: page 10

Land conflict in Indonesia leads to religious tension

- External affairs: page 6

EUROPEAN AFFAIRS 2, 3, 7
EXTERNAL AFFAIRS 4 - 6
OPINION 8, 9
ART AND SCIENCE 10, 11
SPORTS 12
AGENDA 13 – 18
ECONOMY 19 - 23
STOCK MARKET 24, 26
TELEVISION & INTERNET 27, 29
BACKPAGE 30
32 PAGES

IS LEAKING

arch breakthrough in sea level drop

MAY 13. After years scientists finally ved the sea level fferent causes were two main damp escaping and gigantic lows filling up

Koning

e thought that sphere kept the de. Thirty years

ago, former president Al Gore warned for a dramatic sea level rise due to global warming. Until now, the main theory was that the water molecules were affected due to organisms, making the H2O molecules smaller.

However, Dexter Hawkins now proves otherwise. In the image below you see the professor in his lecture room in Harvard. His theory is that the earth is in fact leaking its water. If the

atmosphere is incapable of keeping the earth's water, our planet may well look like the current Mars in 3000 years from now. Professor Hawkins is not sure why this happens, but he has some ideas.

He argues that "due to excessive heat from the sun", the atmosphere's weight may have dramatically increased, spinning the water out of earth's gravity. Sea level drops may still go on.

Professor Dexter Hawkins explaining his theories on a blackboard in Harvard

nic museum now opened to the public

Y 13. A memorable ns and fans of the shipwreck has now n the old ocean ed and its doors to the time. At least fifty ors to be the first

ster "Titanic" hit onardo di Caprio Once again, his the ship ship that ollision with an Caprio opened wreck that once hundred meter

, the shipwreck vered from its s has collected . All the props interior of the been used to

visit the ship, d like before opened later ng will take keys will be vent, giving elve years. the internet y at 12:00 t likely be s.

e will be a se of the e will be fans have certain of

The Titanic museum in Greenland, where it sunk more than hundred years ago when there was still sea at the place

Eu train HUB opens in Neo-Netherlands

"Progressive and daring governance has given the Dutch a unique position"

By Carlo Maria Morsiani

ROTTERDAM, MAY 13. The profitability of shipping has slowly decreased in the last three decades. After an age of shipping, we now step into an era of Maglev transportation. The Dutch have bravely made the first steps to create a big European Maglev network. Neo-Rotterdam established itself as the key node in the European trading network.

The new Maglev train HUB was opened in the Netherlands by the minister of Transport, Public Works and Transportation of the Netherlands. The link connects the important European countries through the Neo-Netherlands borders.

This will finally make an end to the shipping era. The last ship left the Dutch harbour today. From now on all the transporta-

tion will be done via the Maglev train connection.

Minister Lef Mak says to be happy about the opening of the HUB. "The Netherlands will once again florish as the leading trading country in Europe. The new Platinum ages may have arrived for the Dutch". Not everyone is as optimistic. Several small European countries suffer due to the lack of a Maglev train connection. They have insufficient funds to invest in the new technology, making them weak for the trading market.

Former minister Camiel Eurlings says to be surprised by the quickness of Dutch governance. "We thought the Zuiderzeelijn, for instance, would not be a feasible project. I am flabbergasted that the track works so well, and has made the Netherlands once again the key trading country of Europe

Try NRC International for three weeks for only 15 euro's.
Call 0888 5720572
www.nrc.eu

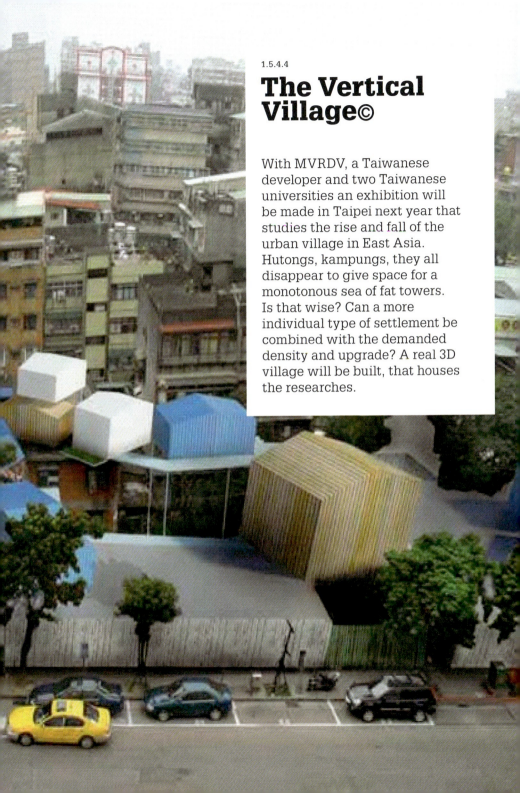

1.5.4.4
The Vertical Village©

With MVRDV, a Taiwanese developer and two Taiwanese universities an exhibition will be made in Taipei next year that studies the rise and fall of the urban village in East Asia. Hutongs, kampungs, they all disappear to give space for a monotonous sea of fat towers. Is that wise? Can a more individual type of settlement be combined with the demanded density and upgrade? A real 3D village will be built, that houses the researches.

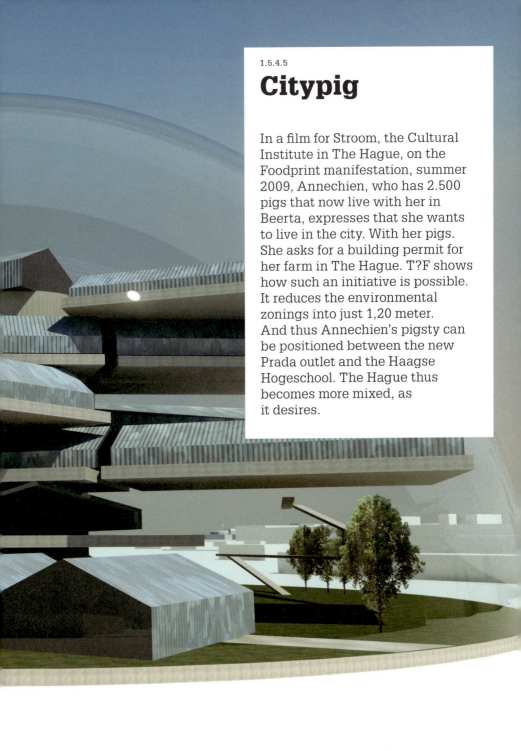

1.5.4.5

Citypig

In a film for Stroom, the Cultural Institute in The Hague, on the Foodprint manifestation, summer 2009, Annechien, who has 2.500 pigs that now live with her in Beerta, expresses that she wants to live in the city. With her pigs. She asks for a building permit for her farm in The Hague. T?F shows how such an initiative is possible. It reduces the environmental zonings into just 1,20 meter. And thus Annechien's pigsty can be positioned between the new Prada outlet and the Haagse Hogeschool. The Hague thus becomes more mixed, as it desires.

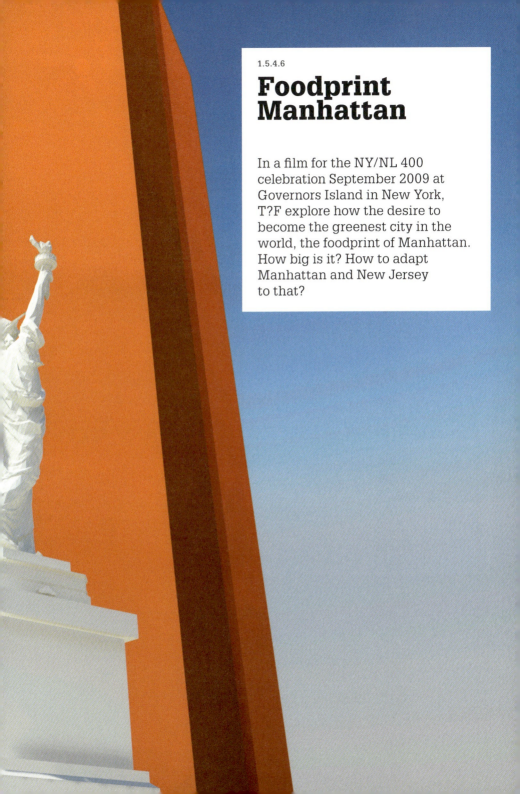

1.5.4.6

Foodprint Manhattan

In a film for the NY/NL 400 celebration September 2009 at Governors Island in New York, T?F explore how the desire to become the greenest city in the world, the foodprint of Manhattan. How big is it? How to adapt Manhattan and New Jersey to that?

1.5.5
The Software Program

How can we store all the information that derives from the model city and applications program? Can we create a library that is not only passive but can behave actively? Maybe we can better store all this in gigantic software, an evolutionary game, that not only collects those data but as well positions it and makes them visible, comparable and in the end even productive?
It combines the role as a 'library' with the one as a 'connector' or a 'communicator' and even 'generator'. It becomes a 'city' itself. An evolutionary city.
Such a tool combines the more collective agendas with the individualistic tendencies of the current societies; a developing series of 'urban software' is imagined.
T?F wants to explore the following modes.

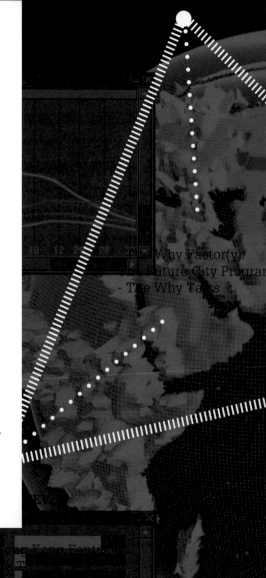

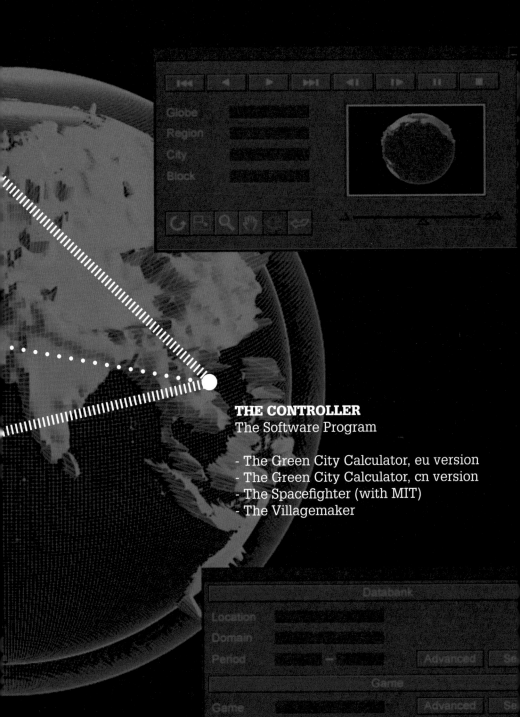

THE CONTROLLER
The Software Program

- The Green City Calculator, eu version
- The Green City Calculator, cn version
- The Spacefighter (with MIT)
- The Villagemaker

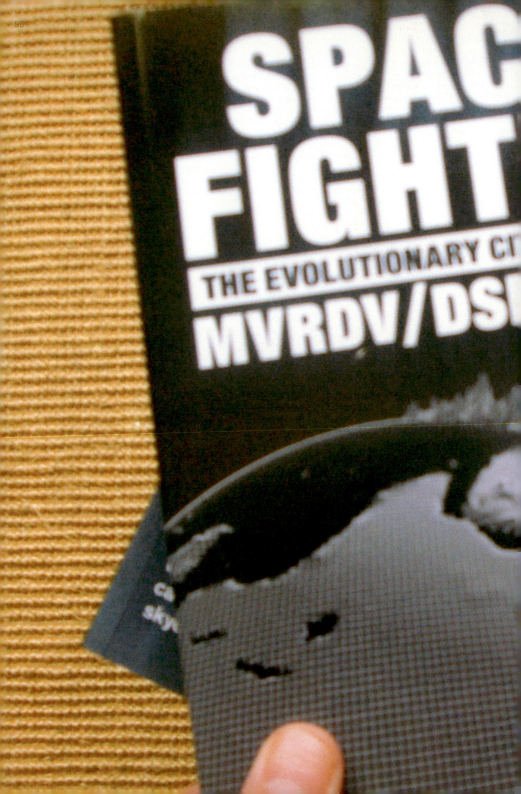

1.5.5.1
Spacefighter©

The Spacefighter program has already partially been developed with the TU and MIT. Spacefighter is an evolutionary model for the developments of cities. It is not based on scenarios (the 'what if's') that dominated the architectural culture of the nineties, but it concentrates on the chain of interrelational reactions (the 'yes, but's').

1.5.5.2

The Green City Calculator©

Every mayor wants to say that his or her city is the greenest of all. But who is really the greenest? Current green rankings are mainly dedicated towards buildings and sometimes to neighborhoods. Still the majority of the CO2 production is done by cities, by cars, by the oxygen input, by the agricultural domain. T?F develops with a series of partners a calculator, based on Breeam methods, that enable politicians to position the local projects in a wider perspective.

1.5.5.3
The Village Maker©

In Taipei the Villagemaker© accompanies the processes of building vertical villages.

1.6. Conclusion and Acknowledgements

With these elements, I hope that I have given you, ladies and gentlemen, a deeper address for the Why Factor and its facilitator, the Why Factory. I hope sincerely that it is able to make architecture and urbanism almost existential…

Finally, I deeply thank the people that made this all already possible: the deans of Bouwkunde: Hans Beunderman, Jan Rots and especially Wytze Patijn, my supportive colleague: Arie Graafland, our Rector Magnificus Jacob Fokkema, The Why Factory team with their incredible work : Ulf Hackauf, Pirjo Haikola, Felix Madrazo, Tihamér Salij, Daliana Suryawinata, Alexander Sverdlov, Young Wook Joung and many others, our communication experts: Nico Buitendijk, Marcel Witvoet and Eelco van Welie, our graphic designers: Thomas Widdershoven and Bas de Wolff, Jacob van Rijs and Nathalie de Vries and all my colleagues at MVRDV that have given time and space, all the students who trust us with their education, and of course my family: Mirjam Veldhuijzen van Zanten, Thomas, Boris and Wouter Maas for their incredible critical support.
And last but not least I thank you all for your attention. I hope to see you more in these premises.
I deeply welcome you to its Future.

I have spoken,

Winy Maas

2. The Why Factory Opening

Dear mister Rector Magnificus, mister chairman, dear professors, students, ladies and gentlemen: it is a great pleasure to be here in this modern space, this wonderful and exciting lecture hall. It is an unusual lecture hall with its open academic atmosphere and it is a real symbol of what you are trying to achieve here in the architecture faculty at Delft University.

To illustrate the concept of an open city I draft an image of my afternoon for you: the session that I just attended was a meeting between the gay-community and ethnic groups trying to openly discuss the possibilities of being gay within the different ethnic communities. The next session I will attend will be about returning the archives of Suriname to the government of Suriname. So here, in-between, I have joined your discussion about the concept of living in the city. This is of course all part of city life, we are moving from one issue to the next, at a high speed.

The title of Winy Maas' installment lecture is "My Future City", and that is in line with a debate we recently had in Amsterdam. The International Architecture Biennale Rotterdam was visiting and we had the pleasure to host a lecture by the philosopher professor Sloterdijk on the same issue. I had the opportunity to discuss some of these ideas with him. I find it truly exciting, especially to discuss the statement of The Why Factory: "We Make Future Cities". It is an interesting idea, on the one hand Open Cities and on the other hand 'making cities'. Is not there a paradox? Because when you make a city, you are making lives. You are determining where people live, how they recreate, where they work, how they get to work, how they lay out their lives. That is a very authoritarian thing to do. It is close to various outdated philosophies where an elite draws out the life of the people. I think the contemporary way of thinking would not support this. We want to be open, we want to create the possibility for people to live their own life, rather than to lay out their life for them. In an open city people create their own life, if we make a city we make their life; so how can we make an open city?

>

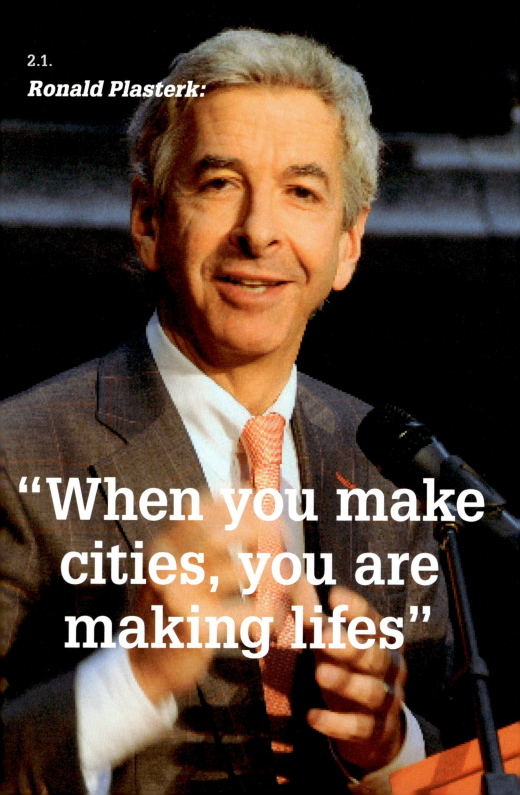

2.1.
Ronald Plasterk:

"When you make cities, you are making lifes"

So here is the paradox - somebody nevertheless has to design these cities and how are you going to do that? An open city demands an open design in which citizens can constantly design their own lives and are not limited but supported by the cities that are laid out for them. Let me compare it to the following: I am sure you all organized parties in your own home where you tried to predict and steer behavior; "well, let's put the chairs here, so people can sit here". At the end of the day they never do that. They always end up hanging out in the kitchen, or do something else unexpected, hang out in precisely the room where they weren't supposed to be.

I think it is exactly the same with cities. You are designing them, but you don't know how everyone will live twenty years from now. The Bijlmer was designed with an entirely different reality in mind. This is a mayor challenge. It will be exciting to see what you can do in this exciting field with your program. As more than half of the global population will be living in cities in the years to come, it will be a mayor challenge. I am sure the Faculty of Architecture here in Delft will be able to contribute greatly to it.

>

It is also nice to be here because of recent events. It was the thirteenth of May 2008 that the Faculty of Architecture burned down. I remember one image vividly: there were firefighters carrying the chairs out of the building while it was still burning. Besides the horror I felt about the fire I found the image both moving and exciting, because you had Rietveld chairs and other priceless objects just standing there on the street, on the pavement, in an exhibition that you will never be able to see again in your life. They stood there without any protection. If it would have started to rain, it all would have been wet! It was touching, there were these big firefighters, all sweaty, risking their lives - all for this stupid old furniture. You could read on their faces an expression of 'why are we doing this for these old chairs.' Not necessarily realizing how valuable the collection is!

I also will never forget the way the Board of the University responded and managed within weeks to restore the teaching program. I greatly admire the way the entire community here in Delft has been able to deal with the situation. The new building for the Faculty of Architecture, being famous as it is, also needs to be something exceptional. As you know, I decided to contribute funding. I am curious to see what will come out of this! Congratulations with the progress you have made here today. I hope the students will have a great time here, and at the same time be learning a lot. Thank you very much.

3. My Future City is...(1)

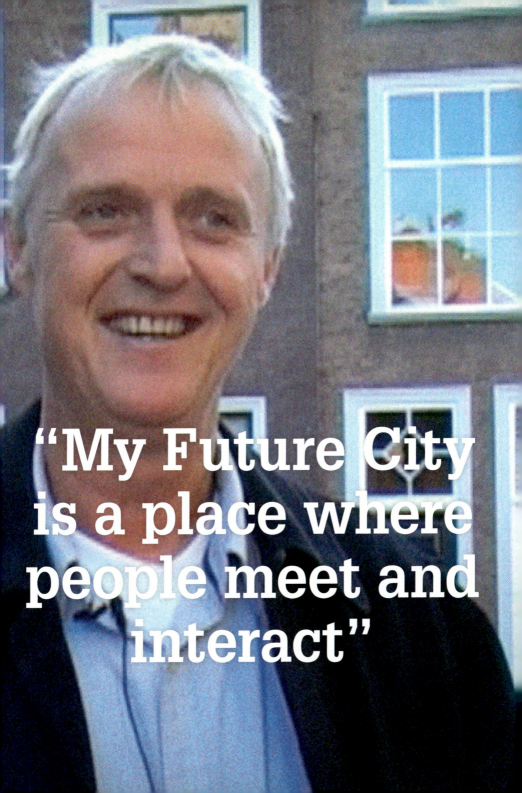
"My Future City is a place where people meet and interact"

"My Future City is not only about form follows function, but also about function to follow form"

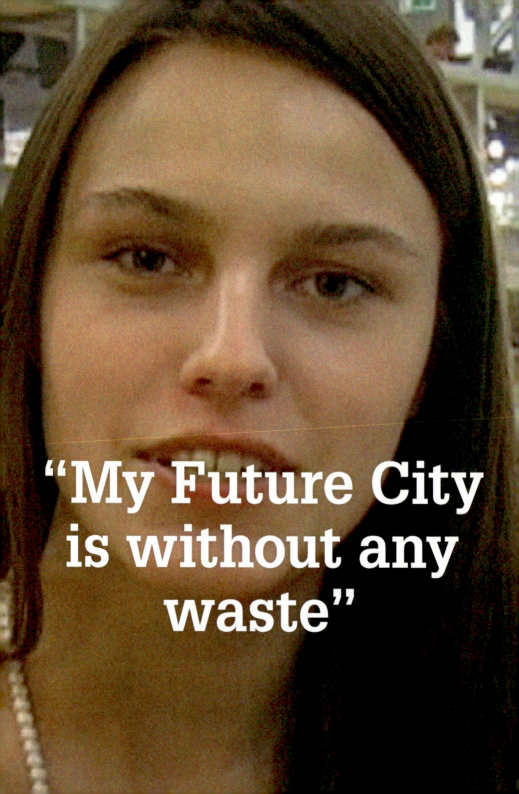

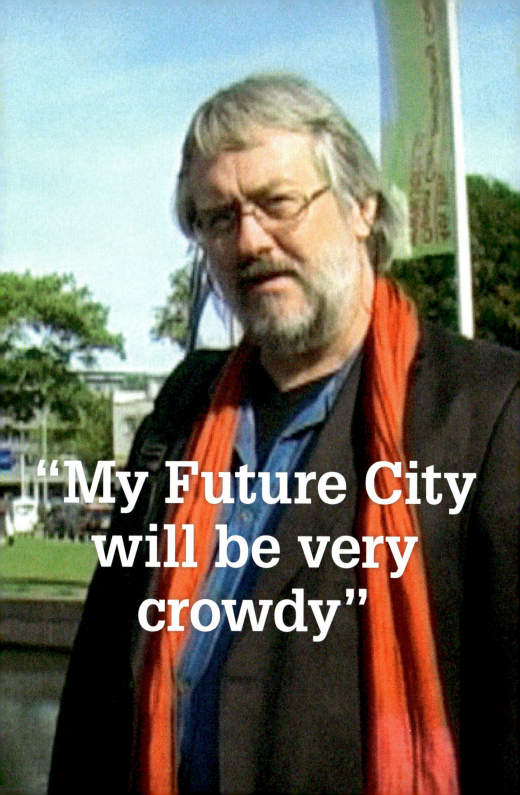

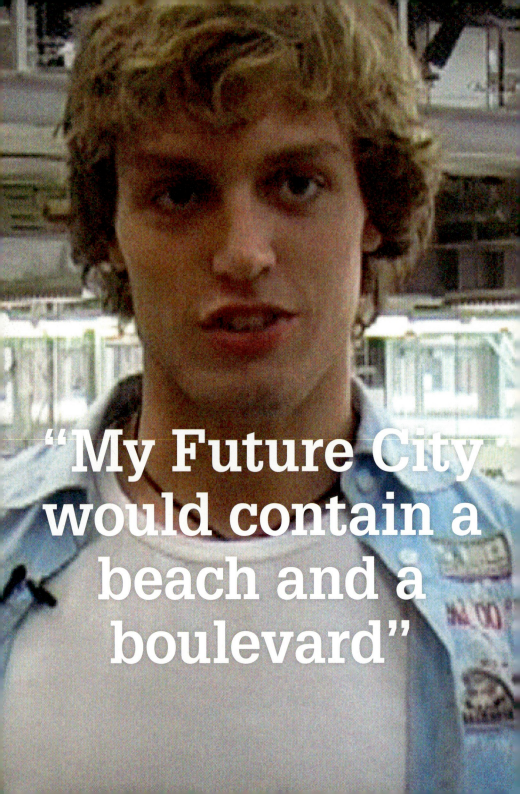

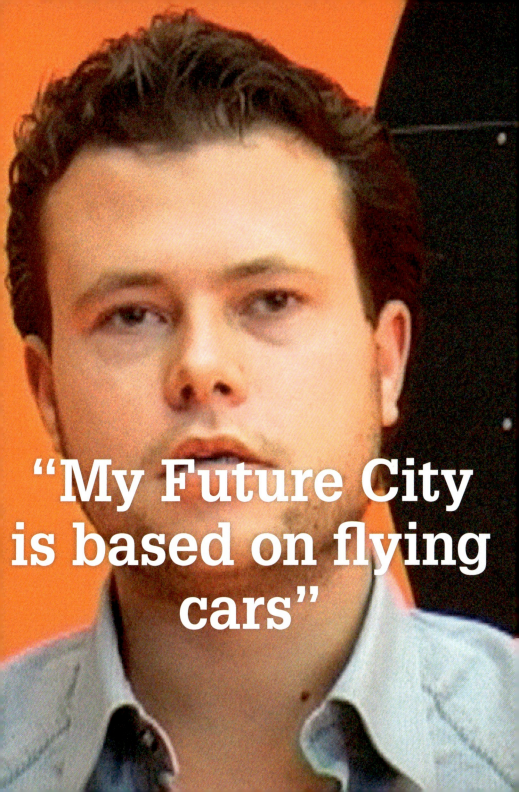

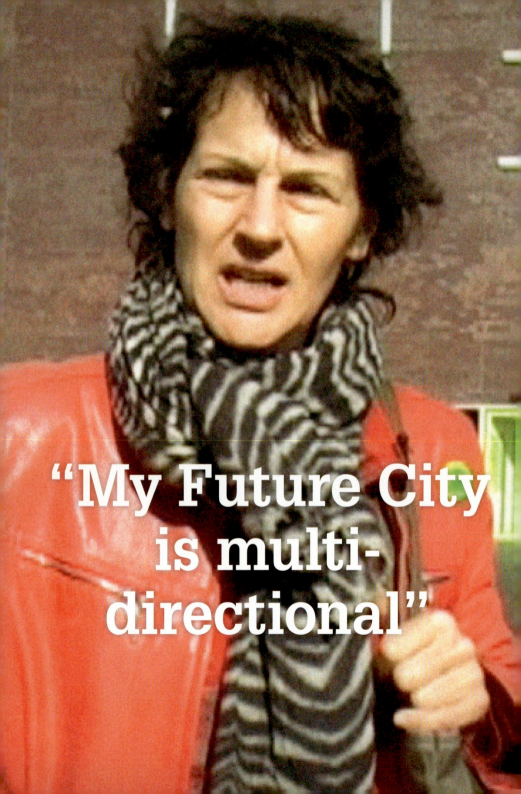

"My Future City is based on urban agriculture"

4. My Future City is...(2)

4.1.
Bas Verkerk:

"Future Cities are not about stones, they are about people"

My dream about my future city.

Let me first stress that we need smart people to build my future city. Architects, spatial planners, economists, scientists, and so on. Building cities of the future is multidisciplinary effort. That's why we as municipality take our task of hosting the university, institutes, architects, students and so on, very seriously.

Future cities are not only about stones, it's about people, life. It addresses human needs. It's also about green, sustainability. My future city has a strong identity. On every spot, citizens know exactly where they are.

My future city is accessible, it has the right look and feel, citizens can feel the city, experience the spatial planning, it is recognisable as well as surprising the users at the same time, it has the optimal mix of bricks, air, water and green, is well integrated in its surroundings, inside and outside, is sustainable, uses all spaces, above as well as under the ground, has incorporated smart solutions for global challenges, like CO_2 production, traffic digestion, working at home and so on, and......because of all this the city thrives economically, is the most attractive city to live as well as work.

All in all I would say that spatial planning is sometimes too much about hardware (bricks, buildings, roads, and so on) and not yet enough about the software, how do people experience the space around them. Are there ample chances to meet. To get connected.

We just started the big project around the railway station. It has a lot of the features I mentioned about the future city. The trains will go under the ground, making it possible to integrate the two parts of the city divided by a railway. The buildings arising above the ground will integrate the historic feel of the city with modern architecture. There will be the right mix between work and leisure.

Modern spatial planning is a multidisciplinary thing. Because of this I think the board of the municipality should take the initiative, because it has the legitimation and represents the citizens. by bringing the right people together as well as drawing the road map to the future.

Bas Verkerk started his political career in 1993 as council member in The Hague on behalf of the Liberal Party VVD. Since 2004 he is Mayor of Delft. One of the focus points within his current function is the international position of the Municipality of Delft and the collaboration with the University of Technology, which he regards as crucial for further development. In November 2008 he was appointed president of the Dutch Delegation of the CoR (Committee of the Regions) in Brussels. He holds a degree in Law and Spatial Sciences.

My future city. My favorite city will have four dimensions. It will have to have sustainability. It has to have culture, it has to have quality, especially in the open space, and it has to have diversity.

To begin with the first one, sustainability. There is one city, one future city in the world that will be perfect. Mazda City. It will be part of everything. It has a sixty megawatt solar power plant, it has a 20 megawatt wind-energy plant, is has water management, it has the largest hydrogen power plant in the world, it will be perfect. It is an example for a new generation of highly planned, highly specialized cities that are sustainable and highly technology intensive.

Secondly, culture. We look at a city like Berlin, the centre of Berlin. Why do people want to go and visit a city? Its culture. It's the place where you want to go. Of course it is politics. Of course there are businesses, but it is the culture that drives a lot of young people towards the city. People want to be there. It is a green city as well, it's got parks, and all kinds of beautiful things, but in its basis it is the place where all the cultural people in Berlin, in Germany want to go. I think people from all around the world want to go to this city, and be part of its environment. Never forget; there is an honest way of seeing if a city is successful. People will always vote with their feet. If they will come to this city, they will enjoy it and they will come back. Berlin is the second successful city in Europe, measured in term of the amount of tourists coming to the city. It is going to pass Paris in a couple of years from now.

The third dimension we have is the quality of the open space. Now picture a city I love most. Rotterdam. I live there, I've got my company there, and it is based on the Kop van Zuid, which is a remarkable place, a very successful redevelopment. But look at it, it has no trees, there will be no tourists, at least not a lot of them, and of course, Rotterdam has got parks, but they are in the wrong location. It's got its trees, but not enough, and we can do better. Can we compare Rotterdam? Yes, we can. We can compare it to Hamburg. Hamburg is a city which has a big port as well. But look at the open spaces, look at the environment. There is a lot more tourism in Hamburg then there is in Rotterdam. There are a lot of terraces working very well at Port City. The heart of the industrialized zone of Hamburg. People will go there, sit on terraces, they will drink and they will come back. And they will enjoy living there. Rotterdam has had its problems to really cope with building a new environment, with making a new area very successful. And Hamburg is an example of how you can do that. Public spaces and public quality. It is in the buildings but especially it is in trees. It is in roads, in 'do you really want to be there and don't want to go away.'

The fourth one is the least known. Picture Rotterdam a long time ago. More precise, Rotterdam West. What is fascinating in the old way of building cities, we made a high, very big road, in this case the Heemraadssingel, and then we had a not so big road next to it, and then there were even smaller roads next to that. And in that same area, very close to each other, we had white-collar workers and we had blue-collar workers, all living together. If you compare this to our new cities, our Vinex-locations, our Bijlmer locations and other cities, we sort of forget, forgot the old lessons from long ago. And in My Future City, I think this will be one of the most important things. let's bring poor and rich together, and build one successful city. Thank you very much.

Coen Van Oostrom is CEO of OVG Real Estate. He founded the company in 1997 which evolved into one of the larger commercial development companies in the Netherlands. The field of expertise of the company is office development with a strong focus on client's needs and wishes. Next to this, he is Member of the Clinton Global Initiative, The Economic Development Board of Rotterdam, and The Council of the Rotterdam Climate Initiative, and others. In 2007 Coen was elected Young Global Leader by the World Economic Forum.

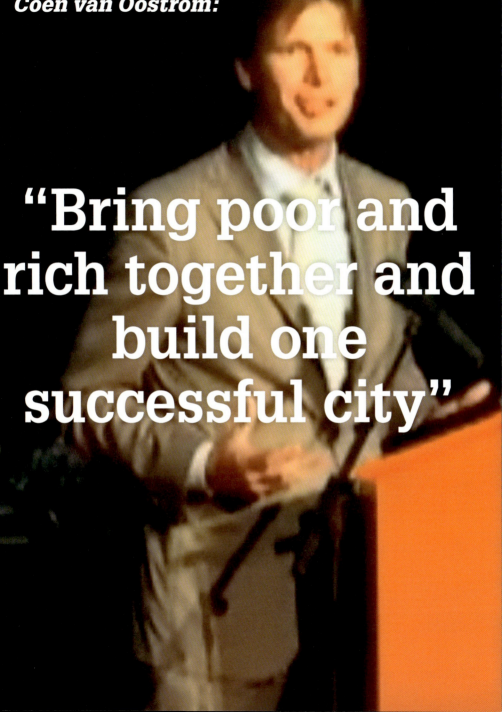

Coen van Oostrom:

"Bring poor and rich together and build one successful city"

"My future city is located in my imagination"

The future city? My future city? What a subject? Not really unique or new - to mention only the "Metabolists" in Japan, the "Gläserne Kette" in Germany or my favorites "Archigram" with their walking cities, plug-in cities and drive in cities. Regardless, the question of future cities remains relevant and challenging.

Some architecture heroes had - unfortunately - the chance to build their visions. For example; Corbusier with Chandigarh, Niemeyer with Brasilia or even Paolo Soleri with Arcosanti in the desert of Arizona. They all failed, leaving a field of research for architecture historians. They had to fail: it is not possible to build a dream. Their pre-determined and rigid city-planning concepts were not able to adapt to the complexities of cultural and social change, to react to new developments, to new ways of living, working, being or even to the effects of demographic and global change. How can a single mind create an environment for millions of individuals?
No doubt: A built vision is a dead vision!
The question for me is not how my future city appears, but how it transforms. More specifically, what and who should determine how this transformation takes place?

I, you, we can only - and this is more than enough - create and formulate ideas, aims, strategies, and criteria - be they social, cultural or ecological - and work to ensure our visions are shared, stimulating proactive awareness and participation in the process.
My future city is located in my brain - in my imagination.

My future city is a unique organism. Like a human body, which is continuously evolving, reacting to outside influences. It has to be flexible, open for new experiences, new challenges, otherwise it will not survive.
My future city is the permanent expression of the self-conception and cumulative experience of my culture.
My future city is "a stage for imagination, its organizational ability, its tolerance and its will for creation." (Richard Sennett).

Therefore:
My future city is about energy. Not about saving energy as everybody is talking about it now, it is about creating and giving back energy: mentally and physically not only to nature but also to its inhabitants, to react and act openly, creatively, provocatively, optimistically, self-critically and with courage.
Nobody is allowed to enter my future city who still believes in the "zero philosophy". With their zero-houses, zero-cities, passive- houses, passive-cities and their professional stagnation.

I would like to invite all of you to be a part of My future city. I am sure The Why Factory has the spirit and the smarts to make it happen. Urban intelligence is up here. My congratulations to this initiative!

Dr. h.c. Kristin Feireiss, editor, curator, architecture critic and architecture historian, has been the founding director of the Aedes Architecture Forum, Berlin since 1980. Aedes is one of the most internationally successful institutions for communication in the fields of architectural culture and urban design. From 1995 to 2001 she was director of the Netherlands Architecture Institute. She initiated the Rotterdam Biennale. In 2009 she co-founded an international education network platform: the Aedes Network Campus Berlin.

My Future City, Moon City

A City on the Moon, the 8th continent of Earth, where people live and work for extended periods of time. It is a small city considering its population of not more than a few hundreds inhabitants, but a large city considering its relevance for society.

It is a City that symbolizes the will of humankind to build on common roots and work on a common destiny. It will extend the presence of humankind into the solar system and advance the knowledge about life, its origin and co-evolution within its planetary environment and ultimately the place of humans in the universe. Its realization will require the creation of global partnerships.
 Moon city will exist sometime in this century, probably in the second half. However, the first steps towards its realization have already started.
It is a truly global city which hosts inhabitants from all regions of the world without being home more to one than another citizen.
While initially dependent from Earth for resources, operations and leadership, it will develop over time its own identity and become operational independent from Earth. It will be the place where the first human in space will be born.
It represents the World's leading innovation centre for technological innovation, process innovation and societal innovation in fields such as sustainable development, health management and human-robotic partnership. Moon City will drive innovations beyond what can currently be imagined.

Basically, Moon City will integrate and demonstrate advanced capabilities for managing life and working productively in hostile, isolated and limited environments.
It will therefore be a place which inspires future generations and help them to cope with environmental changes, resource shortages, the need to increase productivity to sustain a growing and aging population and an efficient health care system to cope with budgetary pressures.

Bernhard Hufenbach heads since 2006 the Exploration Architecture Office of the Human Spaceflight Directorate of the European Space Agency (ESA). The office works in close coordination with other international space Agencies on the analysis and definition of future international human exploration mission scenarios and architectures targeting destinations such as Moon, Near-Earth Objects and Mars. He joined ESA in 1991 and held various positions in fields such as research and development, reporting and policy formulation.

4.4.
Bernhard Hufenbach:

"A city that symbolizes the will of humankind"

4.5. Rob Nijsse:

"Nature invites buildings and invades buildings"

When I got the invitation to speak about My Future City I was thrilled because I am a great comic-book lover, and I collect a lot of them and I thought, what will i do? I will take all these comic books. Look through them, look for the cities that the designers have made up, and which are not architects, and what they dream of. And learn from that. So we started to do that. Halfway through the result I thought; this is boring. For what am I looking at; I m looking at a concrete world. I am looking at a totalitarian world. And if you look at science-fiction films, which I did as well, you will always find rebels in the sewer, fighting their way up. Always disasters happening in this kind of images. You'll hear the sound of threading boots, and will think of totalitarian systems and will think of societies where they make television spots about first disinfecting your hands before you pet your children on the head. I don't think this is a society you want to have. Then I started to think back about my childhood. In my childhood, the most curious, the most wonderful, the most exciting times were when I was playing in nature. And I thought; this is what should happen in the Future City. The Future City should also be nature. It should be respected as it is. And then, by this mix, we get, hopefully, a paradisiacal circumstance. Is that a utopian thought? Can we still save nature? You all see the images of Lagos, big city spreading out, Shanghai destroying everything and making new things. Sao Paolo, a big city of I don't know how many people.
– I flew over in a helicopter and I was shocked by so many houses, so many people living there together. Eating each day, having a good time, trying to survive.- How can we mix that with nature? How can we respect nature? That it is possible to go on in the Darwinian way they have lived for, about ages, about millenniums, about millions of years.
Then I looked into the papers and I see these first signs that we can help nature to get back to our society we wasted. You see a sea eagle, coming back to the Netherlands after perhaps two thousand years,
-They found a bone of a sea eagle in roman fortresses from the roman occupations, that's all. You see a young crane bird, the first one since seventeen fifteen, I think, living in the Netherlands -

So there is hope. We can give room for nature. It has to be interlaced into our city. Otherwise our whole city will spread out over the world, and that will be a false thing to do. Also when I look at my hometown Arnhem. By coincidences exists this local space. But is there a pointer? Yes, that's this part, where the river is allowed to run free again. Nature needs destruction, big floodings, and big fires to start again, and make new life. It is essential. It is very close, almost close to the centre of Arnhem. You see the woods of the Hoge Veluwe, a natural forest, the last one so far we have in the Netherlands. So there are possibilities. We must respect it.
I am a structural engineer. Nature invites buildings, invades buildings. Forests on the third floor, and a finch will start to build a nest in it. So it's possible. Buildings need to be adaptable. A grass field going in and out a stadium. A stadium which is not only for football matches, but also for Pop concerts, Concourse Hip pique, Margriet Lezeressendag, you name it, it can be done in this one building. Not separate buildings, one building. That's the future.
A next future. Being big, helping each other, not falling this or that way, but helping each other standing up. As a structural engineer I find this a great challenge, a great opportunity to build big buildings. Make parks; make landscapes one hundred meters high in the sky. Buildings will become machines. Not only stupid steel going up, concrete going up, but being able to withstand this 'one time in two hundred and fifty years' big storm coming up. Then machines should be able to stabilize the building. Minimalizing the material you need for it. Once we made a vision for a Two Thousand Year Competition for the third millennium building. We failed, because what won; a glasshouse on the moon.
Thank you.

Prof. Rob Nijsse is Consulting Engineer and Director of ABT. Dialogue between architecture and structure is a main concern in his work. He contributed to the quality of some well-known projects, among them the Educatorium building (OMA) and the Dutch Pavilion (MVRDV) for the Expo 2000 in Hanover. Besides working with traditional structural materials like concrete, steel and wood, he devotes particular attention to glass and its structural potential. He was appointed Professor of Support Structure Design at TU Delft's Faculty of Architecture in 2007

My Future City, Maximum City

When design professionals no longer know why they are designing, when their own momentum rather than targets and objectives drive policymakers forward, when process gains the upper hand and the challenges (despite their clarity) are not embraced, then the content loses out. Then passing fades. Procedures and reactivity become our guiding principles. But the challenges we face are too great, too manifest and too pressing for us to let that happen. And to make that point, we need stories and storytellers. Policymakers and designers are storytellers, and the imaginative confrontation between them helps give direction to our work.

Design and the designer have to enter fearless and "aggressively" into the arena of those challenges, confronting, contemplating, setting the agenda and engaging in the dialogue. Politics draws its strength from those challenges, from the place where the questions, the public, the origins of the challenges are found. From the place where incomprehension and incapacity can be transformed through strength into stories and into building and making.

We need to do a lot of things at the same time: we must have the courage to test our ideas, to run risks, and to anticipate the future.

So the answer is to think, do and act at the same time. To act effectively in the here and now, we need to look to the future while also taking account of the past. For that we need effective reflection. To what city does this lead?

The approach of think do and act makes a city of confrontation tangible. A city of performance. A maximum city, with maximum people, with maximum stories and maximum design. A maximum city is maximum politics! Planning for cities is politics and design to the max.

Henk WJ Ovink is director for national spatial planning at the Ministry of Housing, Spatial Planning and the Environment (VROM), Netherlands. As director for developing strategies, designs, research, policy making and their implementation he is responsible for the long term strategy and policy for the Randstad (Randstad2040), the new Architecture Policy, the new Planning Act (Wro), the Research&Development Agenda for spatial planning and for Design and Politics and for the Dutch Olympic Strategy (Olympic Plan 2028).

4.6.
Henk Ovink:

"Design and the designer have to enter fearless and aggressively into the arena"

4.7.
Ronald Wall:

"My system will increase competition between cities"

Towards a Heterarchic Urban System

What I'm most interested in is actually the relationship between economics and urban development; you could say globalization and urbanization. My main fascination is not so much the particular cities and the visions needed for that, I think that's basically up to many people to decide on what a city must become. To me what is more interesting is the urban system. What is the urban system today? Well it's a hierarchic system that I'll show you, and can we challenge that system in the future by changing our cities?

The type of analysis I did, basically grew out of data research at MVRDV and maybe I took it a bit too far and became an economist but the important thing is I keep the spatial side in the economics. So what you see here is a software-simulation of the world economy as it is today. It's a corporate network of multinationals and their investments to firms around the world and it represents fifty percent of the world economy. So what you see is a real simulation of the economy. What you also see there is a hierarchy. The North-American agglomeration, European agglomeration and the Pacific-Asian agglomeration. And those three claim ninety five percent of all economic relations, while the majority of the world population doesn't profit from it. So Africa for instance doesn't' profit from it. It has one percent of that connection. Of course these analysis can take you deeper to deeper levels, the important thing is that there is a strong relationship between the strength of connectivity, corporate relations and the performance of a city in its economic, urban and environmental development. Almost a one–on-one relationship.

Another important discovery in my research is that eighty percent of a city's development is determined by its relationships to other cities and only twenty percent within the boundaries within the city. So we have to change our perception of how to develop a city. The hierarchy of the world is such; this is a cross-section of the world, in which you have the usual suspects. New York, London, Paris and Tokyo, they claim twenty five percent of all corporate investments in the world. So these cities are obvious very prestigious cities, but they also reflect that in their urban development. If you look at it with special software-techniques you discover patterns. And the most important pattern is basically these spider-like star shapes that are symbols you could say of hierarchy. There is the city like Paris which commands other cities in economic relationships and there is only very little interaction which is what they call heterarchic which means there is a reciprocative relationship between them. So you can say this part is the most liberated part of the world and the rest is pretty much dominant or hegemonic. Simply said; this is the world we live in today, the world dominated by a core, which commands other cities, and my Future Dream is a world system which at least approaches a heterarchy which is, you could say, the world in a universal type of relationship, a corporate relationship in the world.

I don't know if I have much time, but this is the menu how to do that, I'll try to do it very quickly tell you five years of research. This is the hierarchic world. Let's imagine there were only tree cities. They are the cores. And Paris and London, let's imagine they are competitors you discover from the analysis. So what can a city learn from this. A city like Paris can look at what little cities London is working with, and what type of economies, what kind of functions. And from that, it can start to plan and program its cities to compete. So as you can see here, Paris, will start making connections to the satellites of London. Of course this will happen all around the world. What that does, it increases competition between cities, which improves the urban development. And at that point you can say that Winy's research and my research connect. Thank you.

Ronald Wall is a scientific coordinator at the Dutch Organization for Scientific Research (NOW), principal of the research/design practice WALL and guest professor at the Berlage Institute. In 2009 he received his PhD in economic geography from the Faculty of Economics Sciences, Erasmus University Rotterdam with his thesis titled 'Netscape. Cities and Global Corporate Networks'.

Ole Bouman is director of the Netherlands Architecture Institute, NAi, Rotterdam, since 2007. With a background in cultural and architectural history, he works as a curator and consultant in the fields of architecture, visual culture and politics. At present he is editor-in-chief of the journal Volume, (produced by Stichting Archis, AMO and Columbia University). He is co-author of the encyclopaedia The Invisible in Architecture (1994) and has curated exhibitions for the Milan Triennale, Manifesta 3, and Museum Boijmans Van Beuningen.

4.8.
Ole Bouman:

"Young people are the residents of the City of Virtue; A city already existing within the realm of our ambition"

"We do not believe in big plans, we believe in creating facts on the ground"

1
Our city imagines how it should be, but does it understand what it already is?

2
Our city believes in the market and in the process management, and in visionary plans and communication strategies, but does it believe in itself?

3
Urban planning should be used to emancipate cities, not to remove and replace them.

4
Reality, the sum of all that came before, is a source infinitely richer than the ideal constructed concept.

5
Taking away physical boundaries, building shared spaces, restoring connections, revealing unexpected panoramas, lays the groundwork for an open city.

6
We cannot afford to wait for the restoration of the big government, now is the time to build site-specific coalitions.

7
We do not believe in big plans, we believe in creating facts on the ground.

Wouter Vanstiphout is partner of Crimson Architectural Historians, a company based in Rotterdam, which engages with the practice and theory of urban planning. In 2001, under the name of WiMBy! (Welcome into my Backyard) he worked together with the foundation 'Internationale Bouwtentoonstelling Rotterdam-Hoogvliet' on the large-scale restructuring of post-war Hoogvliet by means of unrestricted research and development. With Crimson he has curated the exhibition 'Maakbaarheid', for the 4th International Architecture Biennale Rotterdam.

In My Future City there is no sustainability. With students, the Why Factory imagined how we could get out of todays green, what that future would look like, and visualize a more positive future. For me, green today is like the phone booth. It is old fashioned, part of an inefficient system, best we had at the time, but eventually to be replaced by something more elegant. That will happen to green in the future.
And that future is amazing.
A future farm, where plants grow in air, with artificial light and in completely controlled environment. With advanced hydroponic method, they use less water, less pesticides, less fertilizers but grow much faster and better than in farms of today.
 The mouth of the consumer needs to be as close to the growing plant as possible to improve efficiency. To feed Manhattan you need all these towers. Green is the animal feed tower, yellow is potato tower and there is of course also fruit tower, chicken tower and so on...
We calculated that even with these advanced methods for Manhattan we still would need around 50 times the land area. And we realized, some vertical farms and community gardens are clearly not enough.
In fact, the towers and layers we need are so high we probably need go to the suburbs or surrounding areas of the city as well.
Amsterdam today. An image of bacteria in a jar that emits fluorescent light in moving water.
If we combine that with Amsterdam, we could use it in the canals and light the entire city of Amsterdam. It could be known for blue light district, instead of red. And there is no guilt in leaving on the lights.
The image we have of solar energy combined with architecture today.
We know we can capture energy from the sun with quite a simple way with mirrors and coils and store it in salt tanks. Why can't we design it?
If we scale up this technology, and design it to fit its context, we get something spectacular. A new tourist attraction. We get a landscape of flowers that can power entire cities.
We already admire infrastructure, like the Golden Gate Bridge, why can't we admire and celebrate green technology?
In my future city 'flower power' will become productive.

Pirjo Haikola is a Finnish born designer. She currently works as a researcher at 'The Why Factory' within Delft University of Technology, Delft School of Design and as a guest lecturer at University of Art and Design Helsinki. As a designer, Pirjo has extensive international experience, having worked for studios in Milan, Munich, and the Netherlands. Exhibitions include 'Travels Through Paradise' at Platform 21 in Amsterdam, ´Conceptual Design in Context´ during Dutch design week in October and ´Master Pieces 2006´ at Droog Design gallery in Amsterdam.

'Flower Power' will become productive"

4.11.
Michiel Riedijk:

"The Why Factory Needs Another Name"

Michiel Riedijk is one of the co-founding directors of Rotterdam based architecture firm Neutelings-Riedijk. Well-known buildings are the Media Center in Hilversum and the University Center in Utrecht. Riedijk tutors at various universities and academies, including TU Delft and Eindhoven, and the Berlage Institute in Rotterdam, while participating in several symposiums worldwide at numerous international architectural institutions. In 2002 he was a guest Professor at the Lehrstuhl fur Wohnbau und Grundlagen des Entwerfens, RWTH Aachen.

Four plus one propositions regarding the Future City. As you might know architects are a dangerous group when thinking about the future city. Grandiose dreams and preposterous proposals erasing vast pieces of existing urban or rural fabric tend to become the norm when architects start to think. Architects join autocratic rulers to achieve their boldest future dreams. Our colleagues jointly work for disputed clients in the hot, dry or eastern outskirts of our planet to accomplish brave new futures. The future is an idiosyncratic given. Everything an architect plans comes into being in the future. At the same time the future releases the architects shoulders from the burden and obligation to achieve the future now. Or in other words the future acts as a postponed fulfillment of obligations that should be answered immediately. In order to design the future city we should define methods and instruments to achieve our goals, but first of al we should take position. A position based on an interpretation of the current society. In the best academic tradition I will propose five propositions regarding the future city and our profession. I choose my position.

Proposition #1

Planning the future city demands speculation. In architecture and urbanism thinking about the future city tends to lead to speculation and dreams about a yet unknown future with flying cars, neighborhoods without waste or energy producing buildings. In general the architectural future is always shown in Arcadian settings with friendly pastoral greenery surrounding spectacular buildings. There is a long tradition in our profession of so called speculative designs. The designs were not intended to be realized but were showing tendencies within contemporary society instead. Constant's New Babylon, or Superstudio's endless Monument showed architectural proposals for the future city but were to outrageous to be built. The designer wanted to draw the consequences of the contemporary cultural and economic transformations. In Constant's case, industrialization and the possibilities of the liberation of labor due to mechanization: the rise of the Homo Ludens. Speculation demands a position related to the future. Speculation demands evocation of future cities not yet known.

Proposition #2

Planning the future city demands 'counter projects'. Since Thomas More has written Utopia there is a strong tradition in defining so called counter projects in Philosophy, Architecture and Urbanism as well. Theses plans and treatises are always responding to existing situations in society. Many of these treatises like Thomaso Campanella's City of the Sun, Filarete's Sforzinda or Simon Stevin Ideal Dutch City were structured as dialogues. The dialogue emphasized the relation with the contemporary society. One could only understand the proposals as a mirror image of a current situation. The project was only understood as counter project. Not necessarily to be realized but to improve society and to abolish malpractice. Hence the Future City needs composition; a precisely delineated plan to show us a counter image of what the contemporary city is now and how it could alter.

Proposition #3

Planning the future city demands tangible goals. Architects and engineers should propose precise interventions improving living standards and addressing direct demands in society. The task of our discipline is to focus on defining both methods and instruments to address these needs. Social alienation, global warming, sustainability, cultural segregation are essentially tasks that will never be solved through good architecture or urbanism alone. These questions demand legislation in order to compel both clients and governmental bodies to act in these vital issues. Still architects and urbanists have the moral obligation to propose plans and ideas that address these topics. Instead of producing questions we should provide interpretations and answers to tangible needs of society.

Preposition #4

The Future city is now. Everything an architect or urban planner is designing will eventually come into being in the future. At the same time the future can never be understood as an extrapolation of the present as we know it. Sheer endless uncertainties could change the course of history in such a way that everything we know now or might take for granted will be futile after a few decades. A precise and relentless evocation of what that future might be is of paramount importance in our discipline. A lot of changes in contemporary society do not come as a revolutionary transition. The introduction of modern container transport for example is probably one of the biggest changes that happen in the last decades in our Rotterdam metropolitan area. But this was never noticed when some early morning at the end of the sixties the first ship with container moored in the Rotterdam Port. Due to the container the harbor area developed in a complete other way than predicted by the Rotterdam planning authorities. Hence we do not know the future. We should make plans that acknowledge this uncertainty. Planning the future city is planning the city of today. Planning methods and instruments should accommodate questions and needs that are yet unknown.

Proposition #5

The Why Factory needs another name. We are witnessing the opening of the Why Factory today. I am puzzled by the name of the Why Factory. It seems to imply that you have to produce questions mechanically. I would like to claim that we should provide answers instead. Answers based on a clear proposition, understanding an analysis of the contemporary city. A position that is precisely defined, clearly formulated in order to defend attack or reject the initial proposition. I would like to wish Winy Maas and the Why Factory a lot of success and hopefully they are able to provide us with answers regarding our future cities.

My dream is about reality. The reality of people. I am a professional client now, for almost forty years, and in this forty years I invested something like three or four billion Euros. The first ten years of my career I was working on empty buildings, the last twenty-eight years I was working with populated buildings. It started when I became a director of a housing association in Amsterdam in nineteen eighty-two, and I found out it was a very big difference to work in a city with buildings where real people live in. And at that very moment I found out that I was coming back to my old passion. My old passion. I'm born in Rotterdam, in Rotterdam-Zuid, I always walked in the street and I always asked myself; what makes people tick? And after entering this housing association I visited people very often. So on one hand I was investing billions and on the other, talking with the people.

And now I want to share with you some of my observations. The first one is that we have a building system you could say, that is completely in a deadlock. A system that does not provide what people need. It is a rigid system, its fragmented; many people play a certain role in it. We have architects, advisors, contractors, sub-contractors, employees, people having a certain kind of group-thinking, having their own interests, and what's very wrong, they work together, by contracting each other and not by collaborating. Working from project to project. And, what is also very important, we are having nowadays a functional thinking. We have one mindset on the whole world. So this system doesn't produce what people need. Now lets have a look at people. First observation is no two people are alike. No two people are the same. And all these people live in a changing world. And you know that this change is fastening up all the time. Everybody is different, everybody is emancipated, well informed, well educated, everybody wants to decide for themselves. So there is a large miss-match between the people and the system. On the one hand there is the functional thinking and the delivery system, on the other hand a world of human beings who have something in common, they want precious surroundings and they want to be able to make their own decisions all the time. And these are the key principles.

My city should express the need of the people. My dream is a city where this dilemma is broken. A city that responds to the people. This means on all scales, on all levels of scale, a city should accommodate change. Would have an accommodating capacity. On the other hand, a city consists of structures of certain scale levels. Each level should have a structure that accommodates change in the next level. Each structure should be precious to the ones who use it. It should be able to make the people identify with it. For example the scale level of a neighborhood should have precious street-patterns and accommodate changing use of the streets. The streets should be precious in its own, and should accommodate different types of buildings to come in and go out. The building should have, should be precious in it self, should have a build base building and should accommodate the fit-out to change all the time. Well, I told you I am dreaming about reality, and I am a man with two feet on the earth. The city I am describing you is not a city that does not exist, it exists already, all over the world. And I would like to finish with showing you my experience how I found out what I told you. This started o the thirteenth of February of nineteen eighty-three, when I was standing before this building, it was a building that was squatted. These people, already at that moment, found out that freedom of decision is something that belongs to them. And this is what I saw. They made their own surroundings. And this all in one building. So you see it is not about the function of a building, it's about functioning, that's changing all the time. Up until now. So this is what we should make right now. This is what I saw, and this is the reality I'm working for.

Frank Bijdendijk is general director of the Amsterdam housing association Stadgenoot, which has arisen from the merging of housing association Het Oosten and AWV. He developed the concept of the so called Solid - a building that offers full flexibility in use of space and function to its residents. Moreover he is co-initiator of the so-called Koplopersalliantie (a cooperative model for housing associations within the Amsterdam region in the field of sustainability) and author of the book Duurzaamheid loont!

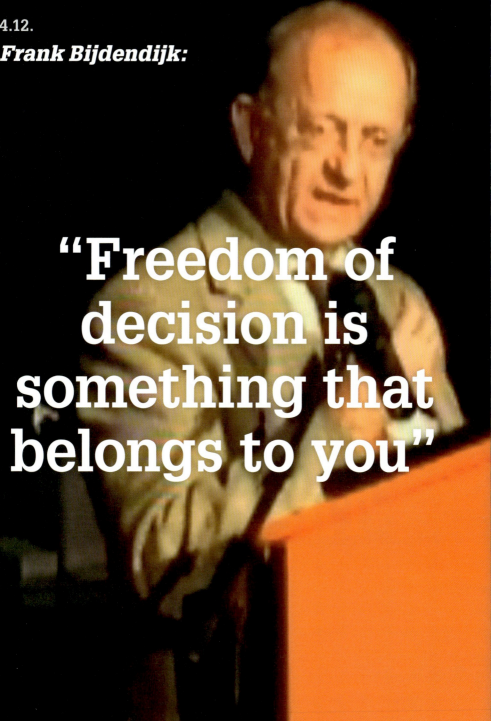

4.13.
Jacob van Rijs and Nathalie de Vries:

"In 2034, the Why Factory Has Been Franchised All Around The World"

Jacob van Rijs and **Nathalie de Vries** are two of the co-founding directors of MVRDV, a globally operating architecture office with a history of creative solutions for urban problems. It consistently builds solutions from a process that mixes research and information sharing into a client and community engagement with an emphasis on social and environmental awareness. Next to a broad range of projects in the fields of architecture and urbanism, both engage in various advisory roles and tutor and lecture at architectural institutions worldwide.

Near Future City

(N) Exactly 25 years ago, we started studying in Delft. Today we show "Near Future City", a Dutch City in the year 2034, 25 years from now.

(J) In 2034 the Randstad, now called Deltastad, consists of a fabric of villages and densely populated areas, with large parks in between. The green heart as one entity has not survived.

(N) Due to climate change the image that was created for Randstad 2040, has become more tropical.

(J) The Rotterdam green roof project has succeeded and is copies all over Deltastad. Although temperatures have kept rising it has become much more pleasant to live in a city.

(N) By demolishing abandoned buildings, pocket parks are created that are filled with orchards.

(J) Solids have been built everywhere.

Green towers are now the standards; the Dutch dream to have a house with a little garden has been implemented in the building codes.

(N) The Koopgoot has undergone a major transition.

(N) Since public space is too expensive to waste, densification by 2034 is a process that can only be executed in a vertical way.

(J) Almost everybody has become a vegetarian. Pig flats near the big cities are turned into vertical glasshouses. This prevents unnecessary traffic. The rural areas of the Netherlands are designated for leisure, water purification and biological agriculture.

(N) Besides the local small-scale energy production in almost every neighbourhood, solar and wind energy is produced in those parts of the world that have become inhabitable because of draughts.

(J) The Ministry of Housing plays an important role in the coastal defense, for example shown in this former Olympic Village near Zandvoort.

(N) MVRDV has been sold to a Chinese company and the partners all have started a new career.

() Winy, Jacob and Nathalie now all live on Almere IJland.

(N) Jacob finally has installed solar panels on his roof and harvests energy, he has become a developer of self-sustainable housing areas all around the world.

(J) Nathalie keeps on travelling thanks to the good railway connections around Almere, her main hobby is planning Station Cities everywhere.

(N) Winy made a big success of The Why Factory and the future of cities is being discussed in franchises of the factory that have been built all around the world.

Well, I'm afraid I have no Future City. I like cities very much; I'm a real Urbanist. My problem is that, I don't like pictures of the future, I don't like concepts, and I don't like icons. People always talk about the future; it's always about answers and not about questions. I believe in a city as a place of freedom. I believe in a city as a place for possibilities, a mix of people. When someone speaks about the future in terms of Virtual Reality, I hear another word. And that is Fuck You Reality it's sounds virtually the same. I don't know why but perhaps it's because I'm from the sixties. I do try to listen precisely when somebody speaks about Virtual Reality, to me it's like he or she says, something else. The thing I really like about the whole concept of The Why Factory, is it's not focusing on solutions but it focuses on questions. I think that's very important for our profession. I think that's the central point. To look to reality, to look to what's is happening in the cities. What is going on? We have to analyze it. The city as a social product, it's an economical item and also cultural. So this attitude of asking how it is working, how the city is functioning, is a real valuable contribution to our Faculty. I am very proud to have Winy's inaugural speech here, and would like to congratulate you on the Question mark Factory. Thank you very much.

Wytze Patijn Wytze Patijn is Dean of the Faculty of Architecture and the Built Environment at Delft University of Technology. He worked for the Netherlands Ministry of Housing, Spatial Planning and the Environment as Architect-General between 1995 and 2000. In that position he advised the government on architectural policy and its own premises. He combined this post with his own work as a freelance architect in Rotterdam until 1998, then became director at architecture and urban planning firm Kuiper Compagnons.

Credits

Editors: The Why Factory: Winy Maas with Tihamér Salij and Bas Kalmeijer
Contributing authors: In order of appearance: Winy Maas, Ronald Plasterk, Bas Verkerk, Coen van Oostrom, Kristin Feireiss, Bernhard Hufenbach, Rob Nijssen, Henk W.J. Ovink, Ronald Wall, Ole Bouman, Wouter Vanstiphout, Pirjo Haikola, Michiel Riedijk, Frank Bijdendijk, Jacob van Rijs and Nathalie de Vries, Wytze Patijn

Interviews: Tihamér Salij with Bas Kalmeijer, Ania Molenda and Ryan Forster

Text Editor, speech Winy Maas: Emily Waugh
Publication Manager and Editorial Advisor: Tihamer Salij

Images:
Rob 't Hart: page: 64, 66, Anton Wubben: cover, 106, Leen Vlasblom: cover inside front and back, page: 8, 10, 112, 114, Jannes Linders: page: 36, T?F: page: 14, 18, 20, 22, 24, 28, 30, 32, 38, 40, 42, 44, 46, 48, 52, 54, 56, 58, 60, 62, 70, 76, 82, 98, 100, 110, 118, 120, 122, 124, 126, 128, 130, 132, 134, 138, 140, 142, 144, 146, 148, 150, 152, 154, 156, 158, 160, 162, 166, MVRDV: page: 90, 96, 102, 164, Wieland & Gouwens: page: 86, 92, 94, Deniza Radulova: page: 78, Mick van Gemert, Tanya Martinez Gonzales: page 80, 88, Indesem: page: 84-85

Faith / Moskee op zuid, "Alles Wordt Goed":
Scott Ponik (US), Dion Lembekker (NL), Jorrit Verduin (NL), Sebastian Skovsted (DK), Nina Vidic Ivancic (SI), Euguenia Yatsouk (RU), Bojana Doncevski (CS), Anthony Janis (US), Guillaume de Morsier (DE)

City State / Kop van Zuid, Tutor: Ronald Wall:
Joris Kritis (BE), Bart Jan Polman (NL), Sander Rutgers (NL), Karho Yeung (NL), Giulio Patrizi (IT) Alessandro Gobbetti (IT), Anja Knudsen (SE), Arnau Sallés Duran (ES), Raja Krishnan (DE)

Archipelago, Tutor: Michiel Riedijk, Ulf Hackauf, Kenny Tang
Guillaume Mojon (CH), Siska Fransiska (NL), Friso Gouwetor (NL), Edoardo Felici (NL), Karolina Kania (NL), Martha Kolokotroni (GR), Sofie Tolf (SE), Stefan Ritter (AT), Ricardo Faia (PT)

Eindpunt Slinge / Metro Waalhaven, Tutor: Jan Jongert
David Bennewith (NZ), David de Bruin (NL), Sidse Hald (NL), Mick van Gemert (NL), Pepijn van Voorst (NL), Megan F.M. Ng (NL), Sasa Grujic (SI), Josip Jerkovic (HR), André Antunes (PT)

CC (creative commons):
page 16: photo by abcgeneral construction online at: http://www.abcgeneralconstruction.com/foreclosure/images/kitchens_1.jpg , Accessed on 14-10-2009
page 26: Project by Étienne-Louis Boullée. Online at: http://commons.wikimedia.com, Accessed on 21 September 2009
page 74: NRC Dagblad, press-clipping

Graphic design: Thonik in collaboration with BENG
Design of The Why Factory logo: Thonik in collaboration with BENG
Lithography an printing: Die Keure, Bruges (B)
Paper: Arctic Volume, 120 gr/m²
Production: Marcel Witvoet,
NAi Publishers, Rotterdam
Publisher: Eelco van Welie,
NAi Publishers, Rotterdam

It was not possible to find all the copyright holders of the illustrations used.
Interested parties are requested to contact NAi Publishers, Mauritsweg 23, 3012 JR Rotterdam, the Netherlands. info@naipublishers.nl

Printed and bound in Belgium
ISBN 978-90-5662-781-2